F U T U R E   S Y S T E M S

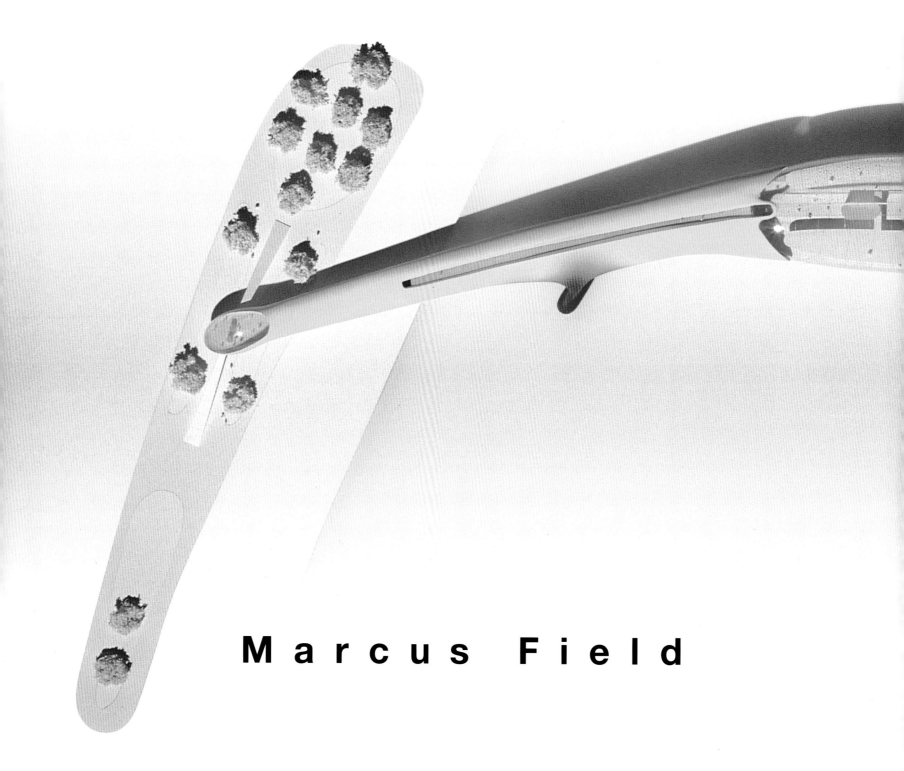

Marcus Field

Φ

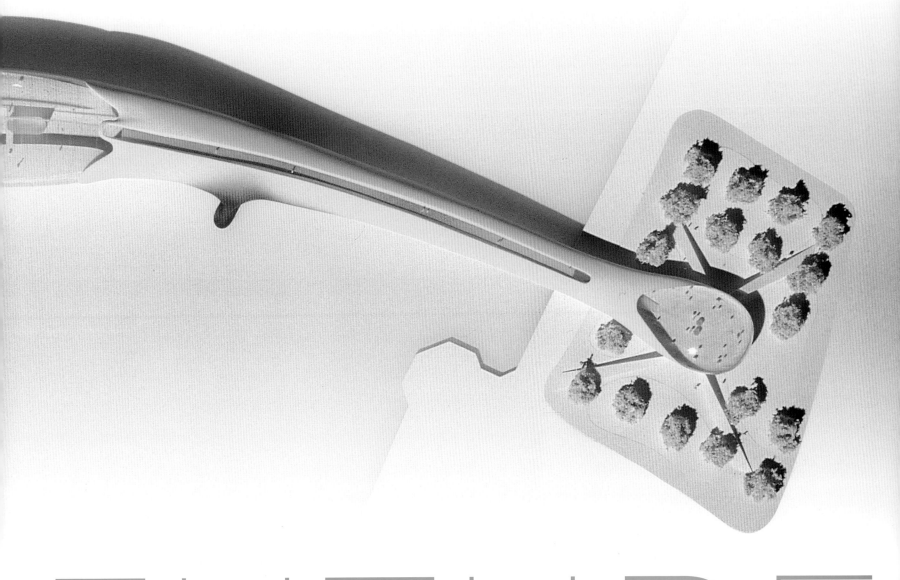

FUTURE
SYSTEMS

Phaidon Press Ltd
Regent's Wharf
All Saints Street
London N1 9PA

First published 1999
© 1999 Phaidon Press Limited

All reasonable efforts have been made
to trace the copyright holders of the
photographs. The Publishers and
Future Systems apologise to anyone
who has not been reached.

ISBN 0 7148 3831 4

A CIP catalogue record for this book
is available from the British Library.

Printed in Hong Kong

Conceived and designed by
Jan Kaplicky, Future Systems

People + Objects • Beauty • Devastation • New Energy • Influences: A Visual Essay by Jan Kaplicky *6* What is Future Systems? *16* On Future Systems *30* 100 Sentences *32* Future Systems 1979–2000 *34* Recent Projects 1990–2000 *36*

CONTENTS

Sketch Projects *170* Future Systems: A History *174* Projects 1958–92 *186* Public + Private *198* Bibliography + Publications *202* Team + Thanks *204* Project Index *206* Future Image *208*

PEOPLE + OBJECTS

2 0 0 0

BEAUTY

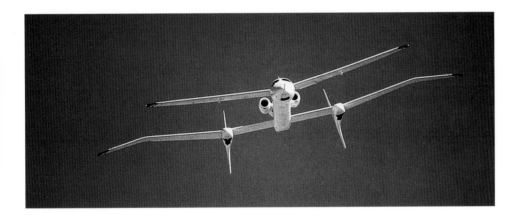

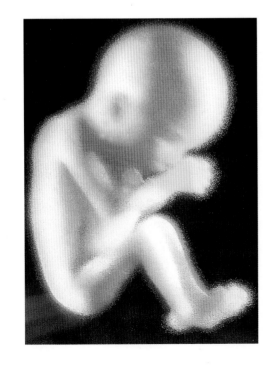

devastation

devastation

new energy

new energy

Anon.

Anon.

Antoni Gaudí

Buckminster Fuller

Ludvik Kysela

Albert Frey

influences

Charles & Ray Eames

Archigram

Piano + Rogers

Le Corbusier

Zaha Hadid

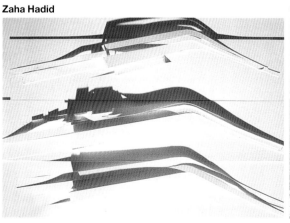

Oscar Niemeyer

Erich Mendelsohn

D & E Bailey

Anon.

Craig Ellwood

Jaromir Krejcar

Juan O'Gorman

Frei Otto

Luis Barragán

Eero Saarinen

Joseph Emberton

Foster Associates

Jörg Schlaich

The Media Centre at Lord's cricket ground is the culmination of Future Systems' ambitions to make architecture which draws on the aesthetic and programmatic legacy of the Modern

WHAT IS FUTURE

'Only through industry have we any hope of fulfilling our aims. It alone can save us from our economic misery. But those people who object to seeing a split between mechanization and the life of the spirit are equally in the right. It is thus a question of historic importance whether it is possible for technology to free itself from its role as an end unto itself and become a medium for the expression of our cultural life.'
Peter Behrens, architect, 'Technology and Cultural Life', *Style*, *1922*

'The Media Centre at Lord's is the ultimate statement for us. It is the realization of a semi-monocoque structure that happens to be even more dramatic because it's 15 metres in the air, in one of the most revered cricket grounds in the world, commissioned from a woman architect and a Czech architect by one of the oldest establishments in England.'
Amanda Levete, architect, *1998*

Over three-quarters of a century separate these two statements which express succinctly the story of the twentieth century's most enduring design challenge: how to harness the achievements of industrial technology to make buildings, furniture and other everyday products which combine quality, function and economy with the cultural associations and aesthetic complexity of the architecture and artefacts of the past.

From Behrens and his pupils Mies van der Rohe and Le Corbusier, to Charles Eames

Movement – including the work of pioneers such as Peter Behrens and Le Corbusier – but responding to the contemporary world and with potential for mass production, just like a car.

SYSTEMS ?

and Norman Foster, this ambition has been pursued with gusto and with varying degrees of success. The way is marked with notable achievements, from the tubular steel furniture and graceful skyscrapers of Mies, to the Eames House of 1949 to Foster's 1978 Sainsbury Centre for the Visual Arts in Norwich. There have been deviations from the path (from Le Corbusier turning native in his log cabin, to the whimsical gestures of Philip Johnson and Robert Venturi and Denise Scott Brown) while critics – most famously the Prince of Wales – have savaged modern architecture for its single-minded and uncompromising position.

In Britain at the turn of the millennium the debate about how architecture and artefacts should be seen has never been more complex. In a country stifled by its history, confused by its dense and multi-cultural population, divided by nationalist interest and fearful of its future as part of a federal Europe, its buildings, art and literature make a revealing course of study. And no such survey would be complete without considering the built and unbuilt work of Future Systems, a small but influential British practice which occupies a pivotal position in the world of contemporary architecture.

A laboratory of design

Just around the corner from Paddington Station, in a quiet and unassuming London street, is the office of Future Systems. There is little to suggest that behind the plain oak door of a cleaned-up mews building lies something akin to a laboratory of design, a place

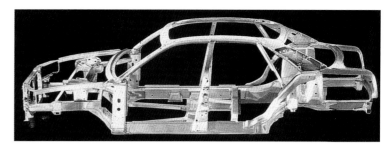

The practice's studio in Paddington is treated as a laboratory of design, where everything from pod bathrooms to exhibition designs – including those of the practice's work in London and

where every received opinion about how a city, a building, a chair, a car, a table or even a book should be, is challenged.

Inside it soon becomes clear that this is no ordinary architect's office. Sure, there are the usual tidy desks, plan chests and Jacobsen chairs, but the bright pink fitted carpet and acid-yellow wall tell you that pleasure and delight are as important in the work here as form and function (something which is often overlooked by critics). Another factor which makes this office special is the diverse experiences and ages of its members.

Future Systems officially started out in 1979 as a part-time team of just two architects, the Czech emigré Jan Kaplicky and British-born David Nixon. For ten years the apparently futuristic but perfectly realizable visions of these two men – from prefabricated pod dwellings to an extraordinary proposal for an office building called the Blob – inspired a generation of architects, engineers and associated professionals. Little of this work was built, but the foundations were laid for the time when, in 1989, Kaplicky joined forces with his partner, architect Amanda Levete, to turn Future Systems into a full-time practice capable of building major projects.

A decade later the result is a busy office of seven people and an impressive portfolio of work. In addition to the completion of a house in Islington (Project 180, see p46) which attracted international press attention, and a floating footbridge in Docklands (Project 219, see p68) which was prefabricated according to Future Systems' early tenets, the practice's

Prague – are conceived and developed. The team has a diverse mix of experience, all of which comes to bear on the real and speculative projects it undertakes.

competition entries – from the second-placed scheme for the Bibliothèque Nationale de France (Project 171, see p193) to the winning scheme for the Ark at the Earth Centre in Doncaster (Project 224, see p110) – have led to a growth in the company's confidence and reputation. An exhibition of Future Systems' work at the Institute of Contemporary Arts in London, 1998, which attracted 30,000 visitors in just two months, reconfirmed its cult status both in architectural circles and in the broader arena of cultural practice.

Although the size of the office remains modest, the mix of skills, attitudes and personalities is a rich one. Kaplicky, now over sixty, brings his experience and acknowledged talents as a visionary designer and thinker. In Levete these skills are matched by a mature architect with significant experience (including five years as a senior architect at the Richard Rogers Partnership) and her own strongly expressed ideas. The introduction of associates Angus Pond (who previously worked for Nicholas Grimshaw) and David Miller (ex-Foster and Calatrava), both in their early thirties, has brought a youthful attitude to the team (as well as crucial computer design skills), while two other young architects – Rachel Stevenson and Matthew Heywood – and an architecture student, Dominic Harris, complete the mix.

But what puts this small office in such an important position in the current design debate – the debate which still struggles with issues of modernity versus tradition, and industry versus craft – is its provocative approach to building and architecture as part of

In line with the teachings of the Modern Movement, Future Systems' work is informed by historical precedent, as well as everyday objects and the possibilities of mass production.

broader social, cultural and political concerns. And with the completion of the NatWest Media Centre at Lord's Cricket Ground, Future Systems' most significant building to date, it is now possible to explore this position and the possible future directions of the practice.

The yacht, the camera and the cricket ball

The realization of the Media Centre at Lord's (Project 221, see p92) is a landmark in the history of twentieth-century architecture. Foremost of the reasons for this is the uncompromising way in which it responds to the challenges laid down by the pioneers of the Modern Movement. Although many of Le Corbusier's ideas of urban planning have long since been discredited, his rallying call for architects to break out of their shackles and embrace the possibilities offered by modern manufacturing technology has perhaps never been so completely or satisfyingly answered as in this building.

In his famous manifesto *Towards a New Architecture*, published in 1923, Le Corbusier accused architects of sleeping while around them the world moved on. Offering the example of the ship, the car, the aeroplane, he demanded that architects learn from the technology of these forms to create a new architecture. 'Mass production is based on analysis and experiment. Industry on the grand scale must occupy itself with building and establish the elements of the house on a mass-production basis,' he wrote. 'We must create the mass-production spirit.' (*Towards a New Architecture*, Dover, 1986)

Inspiration comes from the rigour and delight found in the buildings of the past, and in the potential for new forms and processes suggested by industries like boat and car manufacture.

Le Corbusier's words have often been misinterpreted. At the same time as celebrating the achievements of the engineer and the automobile designer, he also admired the classical buildings and cultures of the past. His intention was never to license soulless buildings based purely on form and function. Thus he called for an application of mass-production technology which would be 'a manifestation not only of perfection and harmony, but of beauty'. The pursuit of an industrially produced but aesthetically rich and spiritually uplifting form of architecture is also the business of Future Systems.

The Media Centre is a perfect illustration of an architecture produced with this premise. Conceived as a giant camera lens overlooking the ground, the all-aluminium shell of the building was prefabricated in a boat builders yard in Cornwall – a process which ensured a quality of finish usually impossible under the conditions of the conventional construction site. But the architects are keen that the building shouldn't be seen purely as a one-off technological coup, but as part of the practice's broader architectural agenda. 'The inside might be even more of an achievement than the outside,' says Kaplicky, referring particularly to the realization of a space without the eight corners of a conventional room. The clear view along the building's 40 metre span to its curved contours – something familiar in planes or boats, but not in buildings – might now be considered seminal in the history of architecture.

Although there are precedents in modern architecture for non-classical spaces –

In striving to make a new architecture like Lord's Media Centre which challenges conventional forms, Future Systems looks to both landmark buildings of the past, such as the TWA

favourite Future Systems examples are the TWA Terminal at John F Kennedy Airport, New York, by Eero Saarinen and the Einstein Tower in Potsdam, Germany, by Erich Mendelsohn – the Media Centre encompasses spatial complexity in a building which is also technically superior to its conventionally built counterparts. The aluminium body, made of ribs and a 6mm skin, ensures that the building will weather well with minimum maintenance. It also has a seamless and aerodynamic form – something architects have sought to achieve for years with render or cladding panels, but with little success.

The pleasure principle

But beyond the architectural references and technical achievements of this project is a feeling of richness, the origins of which are less easily traced. This feeling comes from the visual and tactile pleasure of the work, the building's soft blue lining, its shapely contours, the satisfying solidity of its fittings. It is the same feeling you might get from driving a good car, drinking good wine or eating good food. It is this pleasure in Modernism – the same interest which drove its best architects to promote sun terraces, good bathrooms, the best heating, fine materials – which Future Systems espouses, in a new 'greener' way.

To find the more subtle and diverse sources for the richness of Future Systems' projects, we can look to Kaplicky's declared references, published in his book *For Inspiration Only*. Here he describes the 'image cascade' he found in the magazines and

Terminal at JFK Airport, New York, by Eero Saarinen and other more diverse sources, including everyday pleasures such as good food, high fashion, works of art and nature.

advertising hoardings of the West after leaving his native Czechoslovakia. For him the inspiration for architecture comes from many sources, including nature, science, art, fashion, film and technology (the images from his vast collection which accompany many of the schemes in this book illustrate the point). Like Kaplicky's former students at the Architectural Association in London, the members of the Future Systems office are also encouraged to see the possibilities for inspiration outside architecture. 'I always told my students, learn to look around you!' writes Kaplicky. 'Get on the top deck of a London bus and look down; see the detailing of the sliding door of a van, see the flash of colour from the advertising hoarding, look at all that you see and imagine how you can bring it to beautify architecture.' Thus the yacht, the camera and the cricket ball are all part of the extraordinary architecture of the Media Centre.

Perfecting the prefab

Following the completion of the Media Centre, Future Systems is keen to explore the potential application of some of its technical and sensual attributes in other building types. 'If you could adapt the technology we have used at Lord's and apply it to something that is genuinely mass-produced – because the Media Centre is very much a prototype, a one-off building – then you could create an economic, prefabricated unit, the new Portakabin if you like, but as a space with immense quality. That is an idea we are

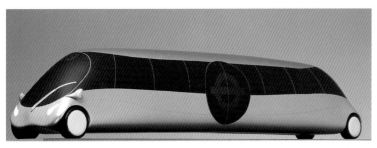

Future Systems has developed a number of solutions to current social and environmental problems, including an electric bus for London and a river-based hostel for the homeless on

committed to pursuing,' explains Levete. The most likely application for such a unit, say the architects, is as a school building. This would be designed to delight children and staff as well as to provide a much needed increase in accommodation. Levete considers that this 'should be an uplifting place to be in.' Indeed, the process has already begun with the architects' winning scheme to extend Hallfield School in London (Project 242, see p142).

Future Systems' attitude towards the development of ideas such as the prototype school building is typical of the practice's approach to work. Running alongside real projects are always a number of speculative research projects, often in collaboration with other consultants, such as structural and environmental engineers. Green Bird (Project 176, see p38), Superbus (Project 203, see p66), and the Josef K House (Project 216, see p74) are all good examples of this.

Kaplicky considers this investigation and research process an essential part of his life, both professionally and privately. ('He never stops drawing,' says Levete. 'I can't think of any other architects who research projects in such an idiosyncratic way,' says David Miller). In some ways both partners also consider research projects and a concern for the environment to be the moral obligation of the architect and feel that such pursuits should attract public funding. Among their past work together are proposals for sheltering the homeless in Africa (see Shelter, p191) and in London (see Boatel, p36). 'The frustration is that however much we are prepared to invest in it, we were never able to take it to the next

the Thames. Projects like these and a tented refugee shelter are informed by mass-production technology in housing – pioneered by Buckminster Fuller – and other industries.

stage because there is never any money for development,' explains Kaplicky. Both architects argue that while vast sums of research money are poured into the development of cars, aeroplanes and military equipment in the private sector, buildings are still treated as one-offs. 'You can't afford to take risks in that situation,' complains Kaplicky, 'which leads to a very conventional approach and a slow evolution of ideas.'

Taboos have to be broken

In many ways the completion of the Media Centre is the manifestation of twenty years of Future Systems' ideas and proof that they can work. What direction will they take now? 'The practice has gone through a cathartic phase,' says associate Angus Pond. 'We had a lot to prove and there's less emphasis on that now.' Rather than illustrating how technology transfers can work, the architects are now striving to realize projects of broad social value.

'When I gave a lecture in Birmingham a tutor asked me how we reconcile doing a building like Lord's for a rich client with having a concern for social issue,' says Levete. 'I said, you can have both actually.' The challenge now is to apply some of the learning from the Media Centre, as well as from smaller projects including smart shops like Wild at Heart in West London (Project 249, see p148) or the Comme des Garçons stores in New York and Tokyo (see pp162–9), to the critical political issues of the day which require architectural solutions – transport, housing, education, the environment.

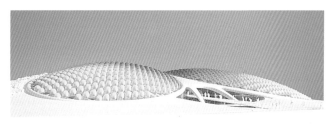

Refusing to accept mediocre, environmentally unfriendly solutions, Future Systems pushes architectural technology forward in projects including the new Comme des Garçons store in

In addition to several proposals for environmentally conscious office buildings and housing schemes, one of Future Systems' most spectacular projects is for the Ark at the Earth Centre. Conceived as a giant exhibition space, the competition-winning building nestles into the post-industrial landscape close to Doncaster in South Yorkshire. In addition to its exemplary 'green' credentials, the building would – like the Media Centre – offer a new spatial experience. 'To enter on the middle floor and see the space above and below and the light penetrating through the roof – I think it will be another achievement in our work,' says Kaplicky.

'For us, the ambition now is to build a large public building, like the Ark,' says Levete. 'You do feel rarefied when you're working for private clients. The experience of entering the Ark will be shared by hundreds and thousands of people who would never otherwise enter a space like that, one with genuine intellectual, ecological and aesthetic rigour.'

But in addition to large public buildings, housing is a subject that has continuously occupied the minds of the Future Systems' team members. From its earliest days the practice has proposed different forms of housing, from two-person pods like the Peanut of 1984 (see p189) to the Doughnut House of 1986 (an energy-efficient and environmental, earth-shielded family house) to two of its most recently realized projects, an office

New York and the Ark at the Earth Centre. By drawing on the research industries like aircraft manufacture, the architects challenge the banality of most current building projects.

conversion in London as a home for Kaplicky and Levete (Project 237, see p132) and a new-build house on the Pembrokeshire coast of Wales (Project 222, see p102). Although varied in form, these all share an ambition to inspire more creative ways of living. And despite being currently confined to one-off and small-scale projects, the ambition is always towards larger and more accessible schemes.

'There is a need to break down the barrier that prefabrication is a dirty word,' says Kaplicky. 'Certain taboos have to be broken. You can't go on housing millions of people in conventional houses – it's fantasy.' Instead Future Systems would like to see properly funded research – either wholly by government or in partnership with industry – which explores new possibilities for mass-produced housing. 'Prefabrication could be incorporated if it was somehow presented as a model that was better and more generous than old buildings,' says Levete. However, the emphasis would be as much on making quality environments as on technologically progressive structures. 'The idea that you have to design to a minimum standard is completely wrong,' she says. 'The extra cost of making a space generous rather than mean is insignificant in terms of the behavioural reaction of the people who live there.' The prefabrication of bathroom pods for the Hauer–King House and the house in Wales, as well as experimentations with volume and

Although the lessons of industry are an important influence on the ideas of Future Systems, the practice believes that its work – like the new Comme des Garçons shop in Paris – is not

structure in these and other projects, are all moves which Future Systems hope could lead to exciting new possibilities in affordable housing.

Meanwhile, the practice continues to explore other possibilities for improving the lives of ordinary people, choosing to present these as models and drawings for real buildings rather than in the form of obtusely written theory as favoured by so many architects. 'We don't feel the need to develop a theoretical or intellectual basis for what we do,' says Levete, 'we would hope that it is apparent in our work. If you have to make the work fit abstract ideas then I think that is very dangerous and a dead way of working.' She does, however, think the boundaries of possibility should be stretched. 'I do think that every project you do, however small, has to try and push things forward.'

Terminal architecture?

In his recent book *Terminal Architecture*, Martin Pawley predicted the demise of the architect as a creative genius making one-off pieces of work. 'What will remain for Terminal Architecture,' he writes, 'will be the sort of pure "zero-defect" design that produces those modern paradigms of technological perfection: the motor car, the airliner, the racing yacht and the precision metal-cladding system.' (Reaktion Books, 1998)

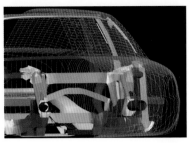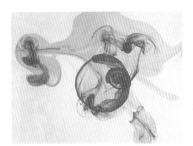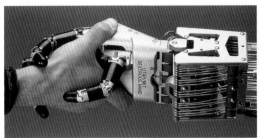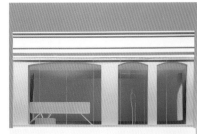

product design, but architecture. Within this tradition, however, Future Systems is keen to draw on other technologies and collaborate with experts to make advanced buildings.

The profession he envisages will not feature celebrity architects and their followers, but a global network of experts collaborating to make buildings and parts which are as meticulously researched and tested as the latest Nissan.

This scenario is welcomed by Future Systems (the practice name was deliberately chosen to function as a brand, casting its members as anonymous participants in the design process). But Kaplicky, Levete and the rest of the team believe that this contemporary form of practice continues to be architecture in the established tradition. Writing of a scheme by Michael Trudgeon for a Hyper House which could be mass produced and sold like a car, Pawley says: 'In this it leaves the realm of architectural design and joins the realm of industrial design instead...'

For Future Systems, however, the building at Lord's – and even the prefabricated mass-produced applications which could follow – is too loaded with the associations of architectural history and creativity to be so easily recategorized. Instead what they offer at the beginning of the new millennium is an answer to Behrens' challenge to make technology 'a medium for the expression of our cultural life'. What follows on these pages then is not industrial design, but a manifesto for architecture of the most authentic kind.

on future systems

'Given the staggering indifference of modern architects for several generations to the natural world, Kaplicky and Levete may, once more, be leading the way towards a redefinition of modern architecture.' Kenneth Powell, *World Architecture*, 1992

'I saw your homepage on the internet. A little bit old fashion, the style of the sixty. (*sic*) But I like it.' Aurelius Bernet, letter to Future Systems, 1998

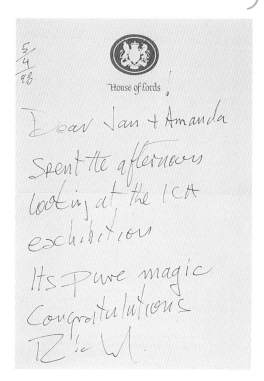

'Future architecture will be animated by a holistic ecological view of the globe. Non-mechanical it will be fluid, seamless and self-regulating, programmed by electronic and bio-technical means to interact with the user and the climate. Future Systems' free-form lightweight monocoque museum structure is enclosed by an everchanging polychromatic glass which responds to the climate.' Lord Rogers on The Ark, Walter Neurath Lecture, 1990

'Jan Kaplicky has guts. No longer need we be deluded by those sad eyes and the downbeat charm: for he has now proved himself.' Peter Cook, Art-Net, 1977

'If any building can convert the cricket-loving, Mock-Tudor Englishman and woman to the virtues of modern, engineering-led design then this is it.' Jonathan Glancey on the Lord's Media Centre, *The Independent*, 1996

'As a manifesto the [Hauer–King] house is word-perfect, if not well-mannered. It is, however, a version of the future that is the end of a slow evolution, not a beginning of a new tradition.' Stephen Bayley, *RIBA Journal*, 1998

'I find your green bird building to be a rather obscene looking structure. Surely, you could alter its appearance without greatly affecting its performance.' Jeff, e-mail to Future Systems, 1998

'It is now apparent that, in Future Systems projects, technology was always the servant of form. To put it another way, it was architecture, not just engineering.' Colin Davies, *Architects' Journal*, 1998

'Has some kind of "eco-spin" unit been set up, issuing the same formula to all its clients? First show beautiful images of environmental degradation followed by beautiful images of own work. Proceed to build up dubious analogies between natural and built objects … and wind up with a hymn to aluminium…' Susannah Hagan on Future Systems lecture, *AA Programme*, 1998

'Just how modern Future Systems' designs are, though, is a moot point … it's hard not to be struck by the retro feel of much of the work on show. Dan Dare would feel at home in this futuristic vision with its silvery pods and slug-like docking stations; Barbarella would love all that pink carpet and fluorescent furniture.' Naomi Stungo, *The Observer*, 1998

'The first true Millennium project … [the Ark] blends insect and avian imagery, in iridescent colours to form a climate-controlled pleasure dome in a great tradition of "green" architecture traceable back to the 1848 Palm House at Kew.' Hugh Pearman, *The Sunday Times*, 1995

'Also in a class of its own is Jan Kaplicky's design for the Acropolis Museum … "What happens when twenty-first century building technology confronts the fount of Classical architecture?" … The answer appears to be a primitive – visually at least – formless blob in strange contrast with the strong geometry of the ancient building. Is this progress?' Astragal, *Architects' Journal*, 1990

'[The House in Wales] was an army hut with a view. Now it is becoming an "elegant cave" … It has to be one of the most beautiful picture windows in the world.' Anne Treneman, *The Independent*, 1998

'Had Kaplicky not been granted refugee status … the world's most historic cricket ground would never have been home to his eye-catching design, resembling an extra-terrestrial gherkin …' Richard Hobson, *The Times*, 1999

'[The Media Centre] is the key to the Future Systems upgrade to first class. A semi-mythical beast, half boat, half gazing eye, it has at last become believable. As a result it increasingly urgently calls for the delivery of an opinion by every pundit in the land … The ayes have got in early and the noes can't think of anything clever to say.' Martin Pawley, *Architects' Journal*, 1998

'Kaplicky has remained un-English in his determination to associate only with the believers in the pure architecture of production and technical invention.' Peter Cook, Art-Net, 1977

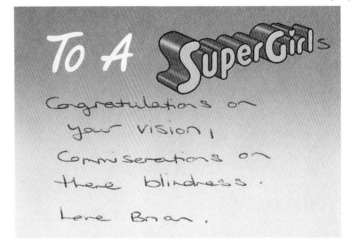

'The first thing you see on entering this exhibition [at the ICA, 1998] is an extraordinary rainbow-coloured phallus called Green Bird … A Brancusi sculpture is not the first thing you think of.' Colin Davies, *Architects' Journal*, 1998

'I like Future Systems. There's a nice lack of compromise in an architectural practice with such a name. The anonymity implies scientific objectivity, just as the implication of a systematic approach to building design promises technically precise release from antique chaos and suffocating archaic muddle.' Stephen Bayley, *RIBA Journal*, 1998

on future systems

JAN KAPLICKY

One has to be an architect twenty-four hours a day: eight hours is not enough.

Let's go back to beauty, let's not hesitate, it is imperative.

Spaces defined by eight corners are not compulsory, nor necessary.

Beauty is never created in meetings or over dinner.

It is astonishing how many 'people' are interested in ugliness and kitsch.

When I see an ugly building I would like to see the face of its 'creator'.

I feel there is always somebody, somewhere, creating something our generation has never thought of.

Sometimes one small image can change our vision of architecture or design.

From now on architecture or design will be the result of teamwork, not the creation of a single individual.

'People' never create, they only criticize.

Beauty – poetry – people: three critical and essential words for the future.

There is only one ugly bridge in the world and it is in Prague.

No good architecture is ever associated with a single political party.

Why not create free forms inside and out? Human beings are not boxes.

We can create beauty in architecture without sophisticated materials.

Le Corbusier, Oscar Niemeyer and others often talk about the beauty of the human body – many never notice.

'People' have total confidence in the designers of an aeroplane, but not in architects.

Beauty is a real problem for many architects.

Architectural critics never use the word beauty – it is not fashionable.

The smell of coffee, a glass of wine can be more inspirational than seven architectural magazines.

People have eyes but few can see.

Many cultures are based on non-rectangular buildings – we should be one of those cultures.

I feel sorry for architects who cannot see the beauty of a simple form; they have to decorate.

Bad architects want to sit on committees and better ones want to design.

Architecture is the only profession which often looks backwards.

I admire brave and forward-thinking fashion designers.

Good architecture always has been, and always will be, a work of art.

It is astonishing how few colours architects use; mainly grey and brown.

In our profession one has to have dedication – complete dedication.

The ecologically acceptable car is coming now (electric or hybrid).

The figures I admire most: Le Corbusier, Oscar Niemeyer, Erich Mendelsohn, Charles Eames, Paul Nelson, Frederick Kiesler, Louis Barragán and many others.

We take risks with every project – others just want a comfortable life.

Designers of a new aeroplane do not ask 'people' to comment, they ask other professionals.

One little smile could sometimes help to create better buildings.

I lived for twenty-six years under various dictatorships – one is probably damaged by this forever.

Every building is a mass, not just four elevations.

Soon, ecological requirements will radically change the appearance of buildings.

Architecture has always been and will continue to be created by designers, not by architecture critics or intellectuals.

Many architects treat green spaces with disrespect; it is time to change this attitude.

Blue sky, sand, wind, sun, shadows, beautiful bodies – I wish I could create buildings as wonderful as that.

Creativity is an essential part of every human existence.

Colour, colour and more colour, not just architects' grey.

I learn a lot about form making model aeroplanes.

British architecture must be European architecture.

Without creativity there is nothing.

It is no longer possible to make excuses for materials – fantastic things can be built with the most simple materials.

What would I wish most? To see five or ten years ahead.

Architects read too little and don't look around enough; they only gossip – it's easier.

There must always be time for a new drawing or idea, not only for chatting in the pub.

Ecological architecture is here and it is here to stay: the energy performance of buildings will be the most important factor in the forthcoming years.

One criterion for success in the next century will be how much a building weighs.

It is not important how many tons of concrete you use in your life; the important thing is how it is used.

When I see a spider's web, I am ashamed by our clumsy buildings.

A return to beauty in architecture is necessary: forget the disasters of the past.

I am always aware how much art is hidden in every detail of a building.

Spaces defined by eight corners are on the decline. In the future, space will be defined differently.

I am convinced that the architecture of straight lines is history.

The range of inspiration that we can find in books, in films and on television is unbelievable.

I envy first-year students of architecture – they have everything in front of them.

Don't judge the success of architects by their bank accounts, but by the beauty of their work.

Modern architecture is not the latest style, it is a necessity.

Architectural criticism is completely absent, only journalism exists.

I will never forget the day when I first saw the chapel at Ronchamp.

We must fly and soar very high.

'People' hated and protested against the Eiffel Tower, St Paul's Cathedral, Sydney Opera House, Centre Pompidou – today they buy postcards of them.

The ability to see ahead and predict is the privilege of the few.

I am glad the jumbo-jet was not designed by an architect – if it had been, it would never have flown.

Personal freedom is a prerequisite for freedom in architecture.

The future of architecture is in future generations.

I respect the buildings of people who built so little so well: Paul Nelson, Pierre Chareau, Charles and Ray Eames, Albert Frey and others.

I have never heard the expression 'ugly aeroplane', but the expression 'ugly building' quite often.

It is not necessary to categorize stylistically: buildings are good or bad.

The concept of 'new materials' presently doesn't exist but one which might soon arrive is a 'universal non-flammable mass for construction'.

Inspiration can be a butterfly, a submarine, an aeroplane, a historical building, a plant, a fashion magazine … the choice is endless.

The best things often come from pain.

Microsoft's mouse can't yet replace the left or right hand.

More and more I am convinced that architecture is made by the people in it.

Architects think in black and white, then they add colour.

Architecture is a total work of art.

I see a limited influence of computers in the next twenty years.

Let us create modern buildings, not modernist ones.

Beauty is on my mind all the time.

Direct human contact stands well above e-mail messages.

The quality of the first sketch is imperative for the quality of the new building.

Ignore popular taste – it is usually very bad.

The best architecture is always poetic.

Architecture is no longer about cornices, stairs, roofs or windows; from now on we must conquer the space.

Democracy and freedom of expression are essential parts of the creative process.

I would like to speak to more wise and creative people.

I admire unity and simplicity of idea, structural efficiency and beauty in nature.

No architecture can be created only theoretically.

Smell is going to be another dimension in future architecture.

A turning point for me was discovering how to break the limits of the space box.

To put St Peter's dome on the top of a supermarket is not just kitsch, it is a crime.

I wish to have the freedom of mind with which a child creates.

The British Isles can't be a museum of the nineteenth century as some would wish.

Complete plastic freedom of inside and outside must be the future.

When somebody asked me what will happen architecturally in 2050, I said I don't know.

I am not interested in futuristic architecture or science-fiction, only in modern architecture.

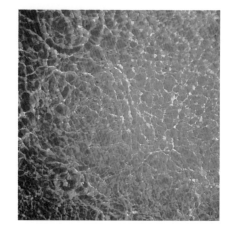

sentences

FUTURE SYSTEMS

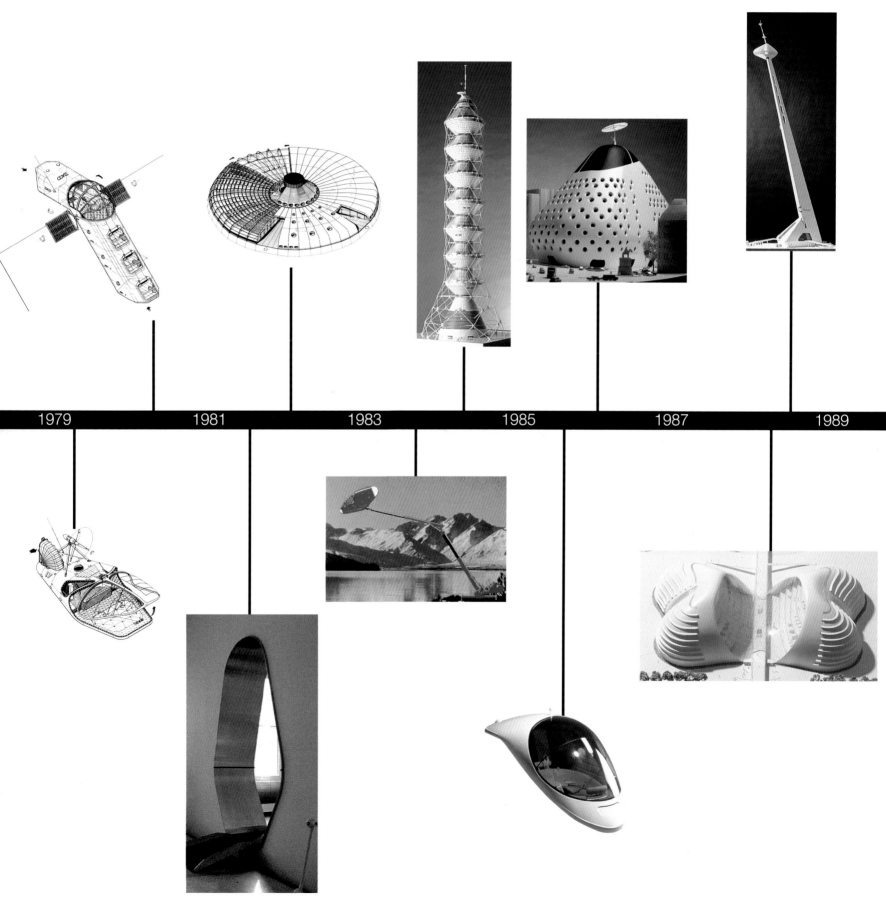

1979   1981   1983   1985   1987   1989

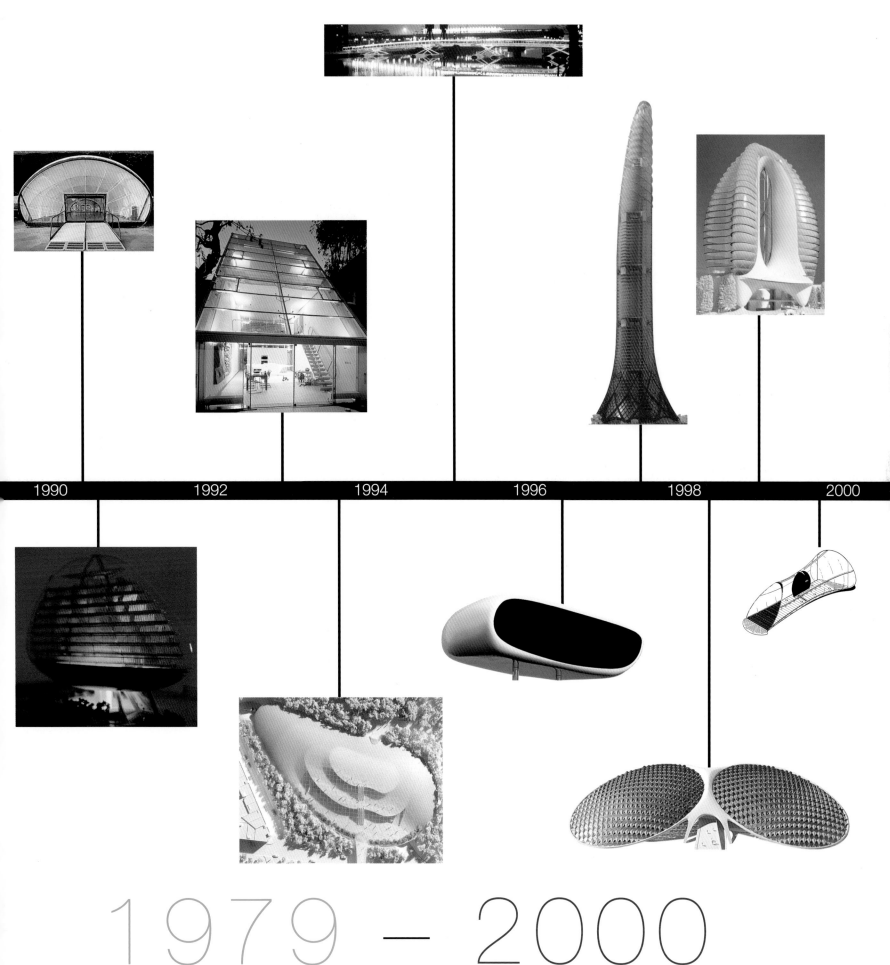

1990 1992 1994 1996 1998 2000

1979 — 2000

175 BOATEL 1990

This self-initiated project is to provide temporary accommodation for 150 homeless people on the Thames in London. It is inspired by the Salvation Army barge Le Corbusier designed in 1929 for the same purpose on the Seine. Among the advantages of Boatel over traditional buildings are the availability and affordability of centrally located sites and the economic nature of its plywood construction (the accommodation block sits on a standard Thames barge). Each room has an opening window for light and ventilation and there is a large area for socializing in the centre of the boat.

Although some charities have been approached with the proposal they have found its unconventional nature difficult to accept. Kaplicky cites the submarine as an analogy; 'People live comfortably in submarines for months. This is only provisional accommodation, and surely it is better for people to be warm in a cubicle than sleeping rough outside?'

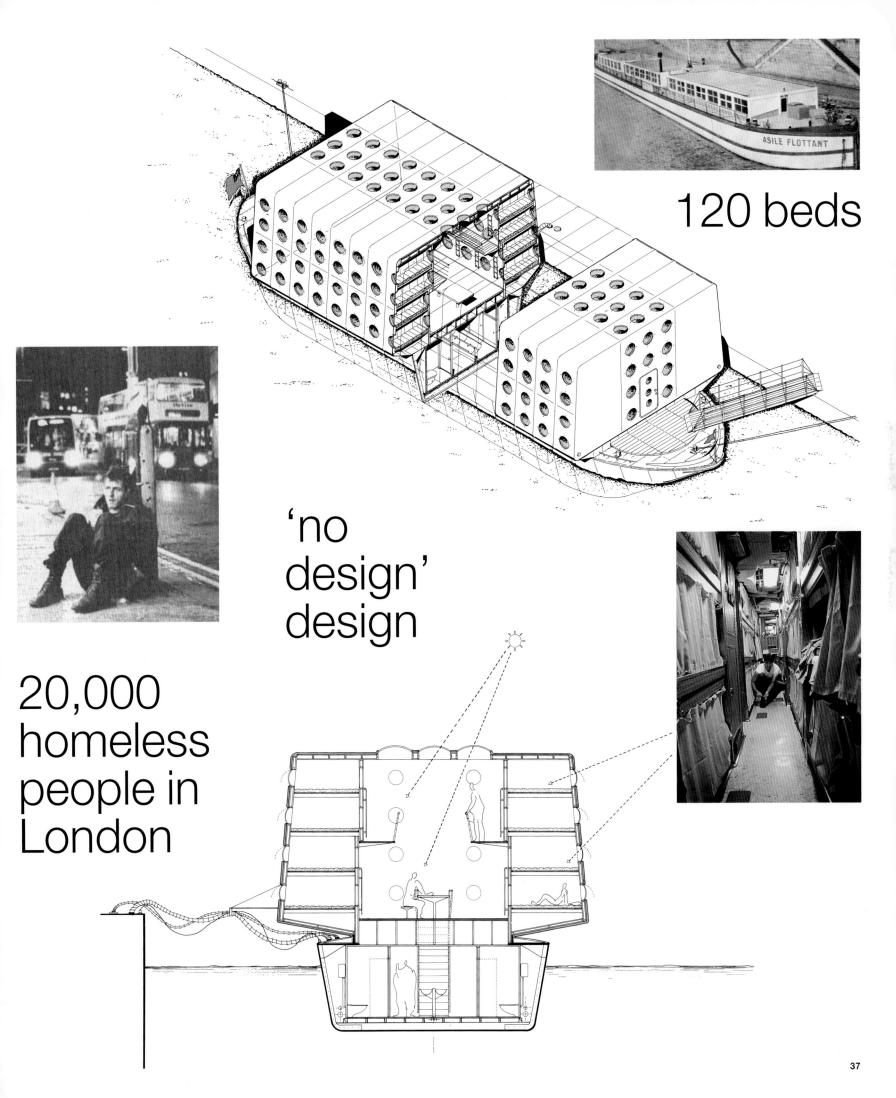

ASILE FLOTTANT

120 beds

'no design' design

20,000 homeless people in London

176 GREEN BIRD 1996

This colourful and elegant proposal for a 100-storey mixed-use skyscraper in London is a response to the banality and inefficiency of so many high-rise buildings today. Designed as a collaboration between Future Systems, the structural engineer Techniker and the environmental engineer BDSP, the building is conceived as a radical alternative in terms of aesthetics, structure and environmental control.

The proposed site is one currently occupied by the derelict Battersea Power Station (effectively 'a dead building,' says Kaplicky). Residents, office workers and visitors would arrive by car or from the Thames by boat. A new bridge across the river is included in the proposal together with underground parking. Inside, a vast lobby gives access to the floors of offices and apartments as well as a restaurant and observation deck above. Travel though the building is by elevator, with local lifts between smaller segments of the building easing the pressure and energy consumption of express lifts. One of the perceived advantages of the building's form is the higher percentage of top grade office areas. These are located around the perimeter, while daylight penetrates deep into the space aided by generous 3.3 metre floor-to-ceiling heights, a system of parabolic mirrors and floors cut back on the north-facing elevations to allow more light to pass through.

Among the 'green' claims of the building over conventional office towers is the envisaged reduction in mechanical ventilation. Opening windows at a high level allows air in, while absorption coolers reject

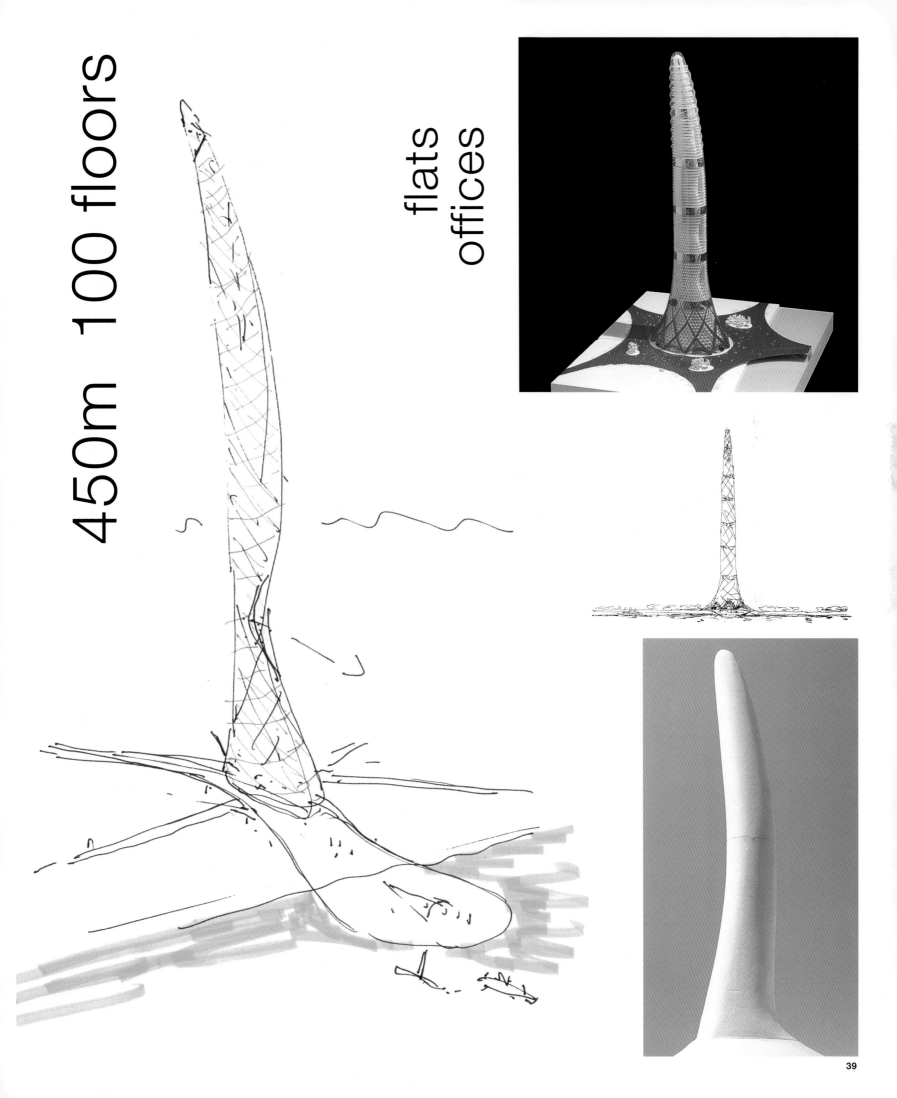

450m 100 floors

flats
offices

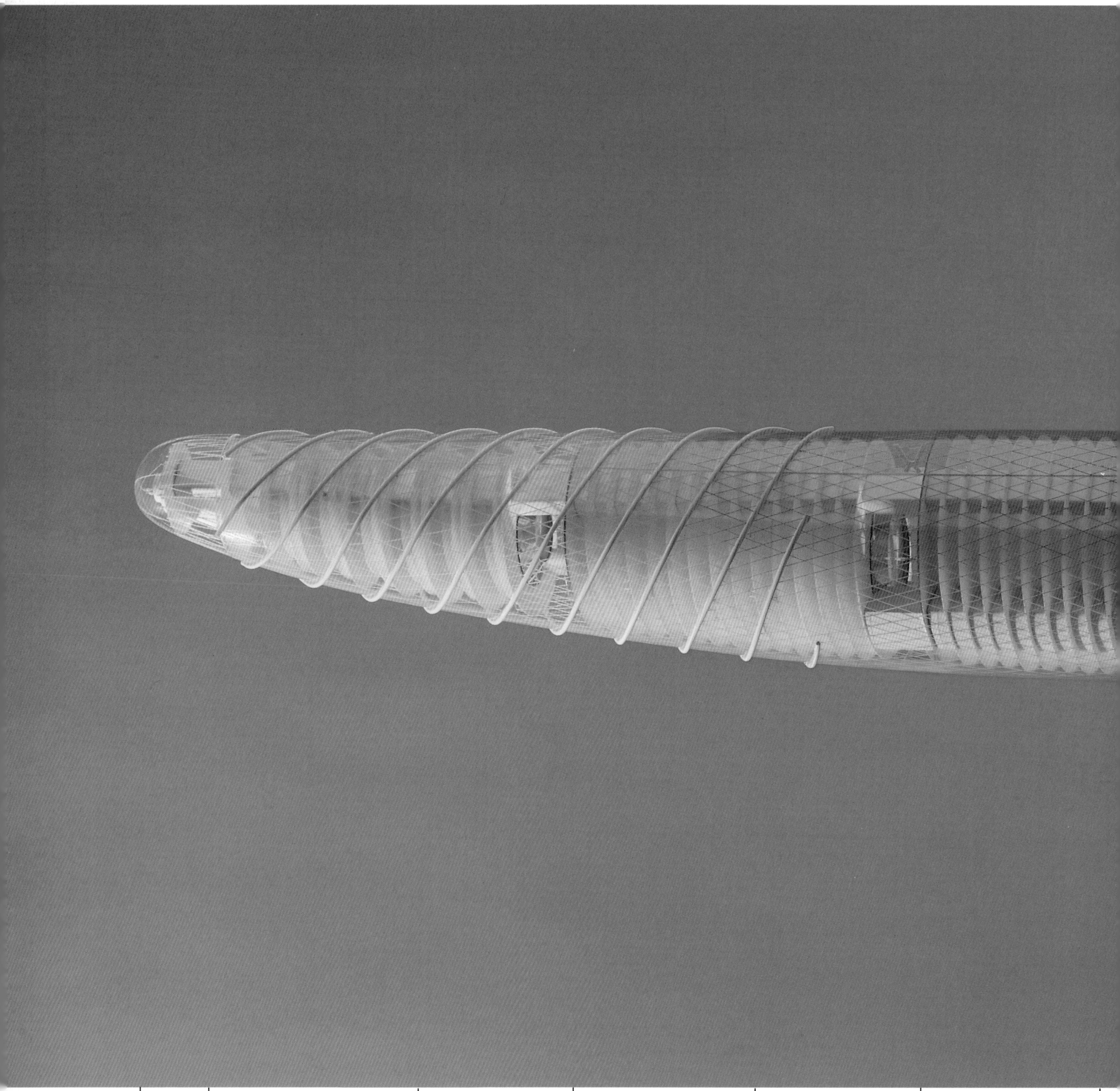

450M

OBSERVATION
FLOOR

RESTAURANT

APARTMENTS

TRIPLE HEIGHT
PLANT/FLOOR VOID

OFFICES

TRIPLE HEIGHT
PLANT/FLOOR VOID

OFFICES

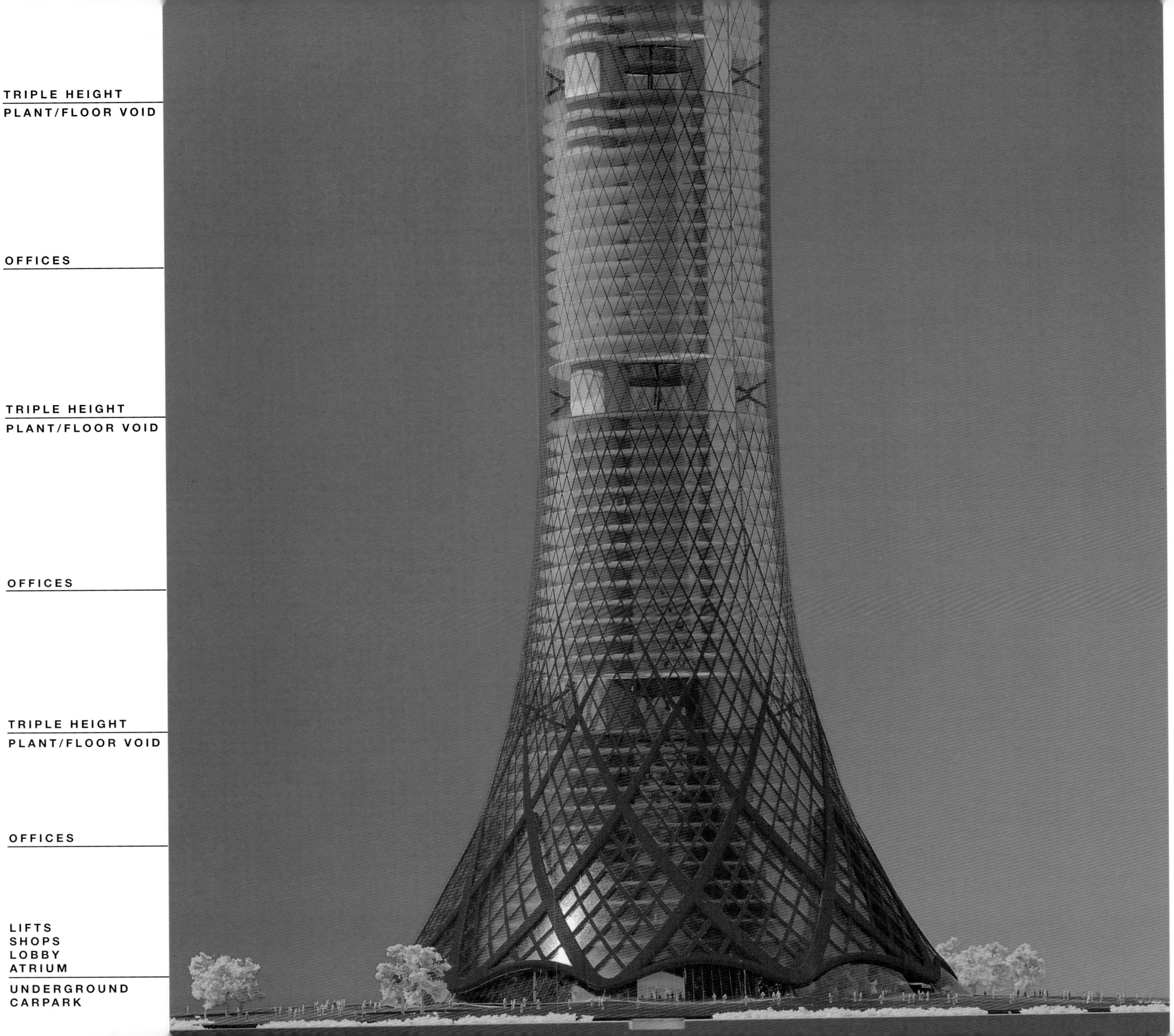

TRIPLE HEIGHT
PLANT/FLOOR VOID

OFFICES

TRIPLE HEIGHT
PLANT/FLOOR VOID

OFFICES

TRIPLE HEIGHT
PLANT/FLOOR VOID

OFFICES

LIFTS
SHOPS
LOBBY
ATRIUM
UNDERGROUND
CARPARK

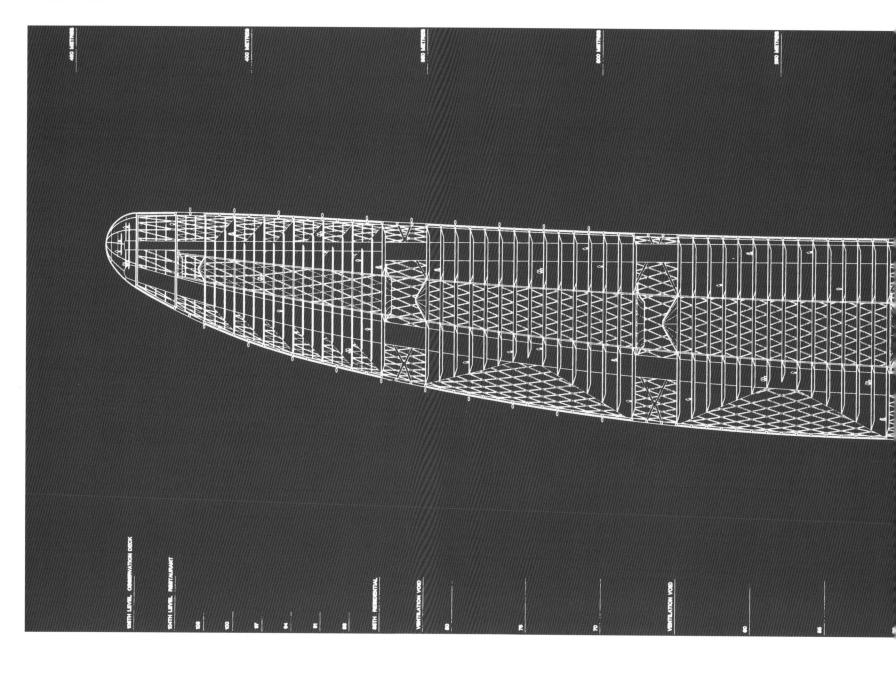

108TH LEVEL, OBSERVATION DECK
104TH LEVEL, RESTAURANT
108 100 97 94 91 88
88TH RESIDENTIAL
VENTILATION VOID
80 78 72
VENTILATION VOID
68 65

400 METRES 400 METRES 500 METRES 500 METRES 500 METRES

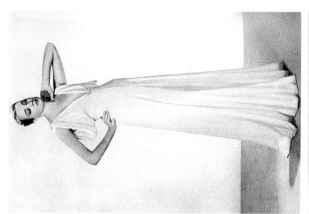

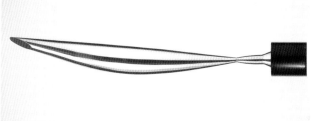

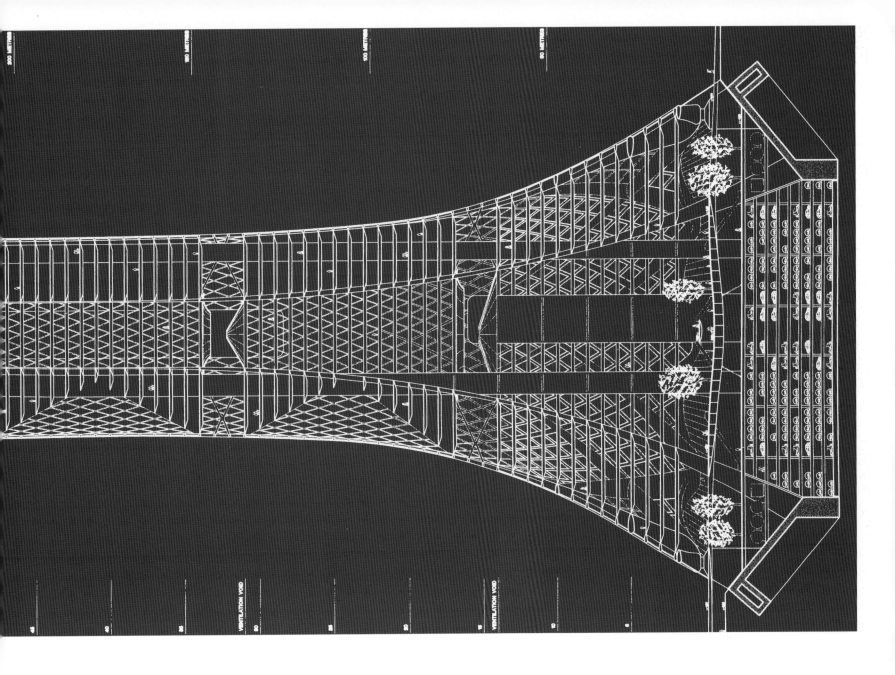

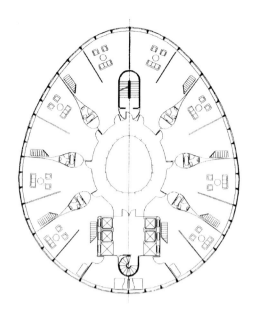
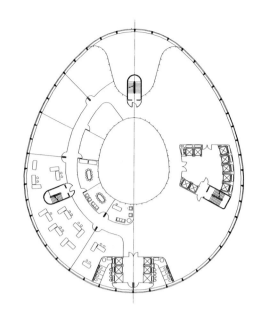
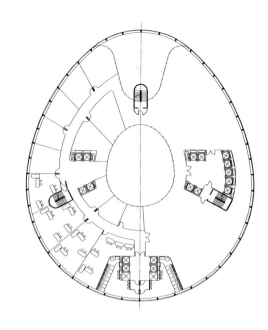

accumulated heat into the river. Photovoltaic cells are also incorporated into the fabric of the building for the generation of free energy. Structurally the tower is formed from a series of concentric braced steel lattices linked by radial frames. The double curved form is inherently rigid – much stronger than post and beam – aerodynamic and aesthetically fresh. For Kaplicky, the inspiration for this proposal comes from a number of sources, ranging from the spectacular engineering projects of Vladimir Suchov to fishnet stockings. In addition to the dynamism of the form, with its unusual rounded top ('why are towers always flat?' he laments), colour has been introduced around the structure. 'We should question why buildings are not more colourful,' Kaplicky says. 'Cesar Pelli's towers, for example, are always so grey. Are architects colour blind? Buildings should be more cheerful.'

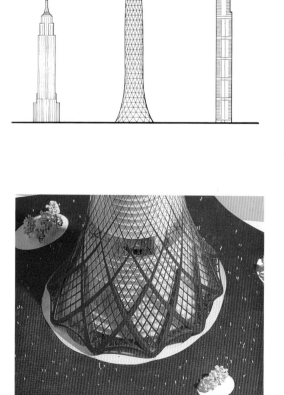

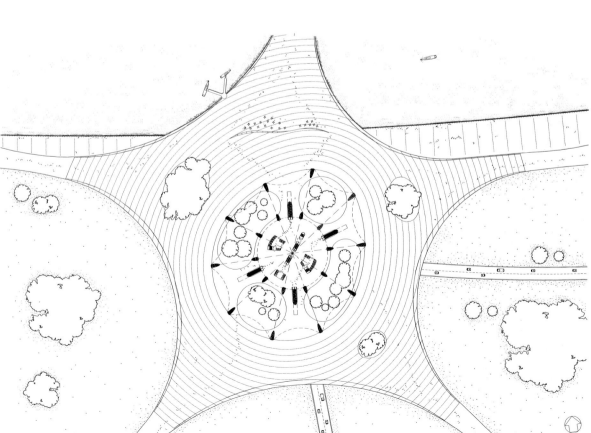

structure
environmental systems

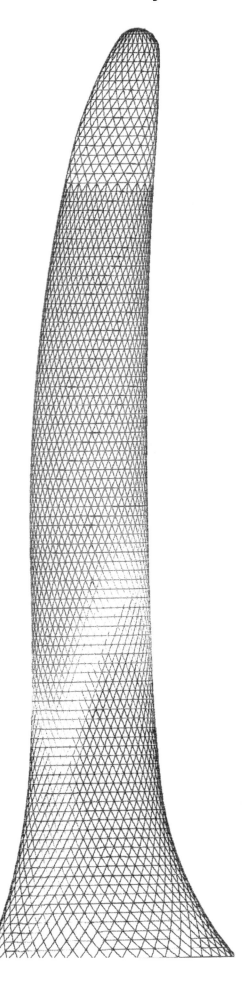

EXPERIMENTAL ECOLOGICAL OFFICE AND RESIDENTIAL
HIGH-RISE BUILDING AND SHOPS • STEEL STRUCTURE •
6 ECOLOGICAL FLOORS • WIND DEFLECTOR • SPECIAL
LIFT SYSTEM

HEIGHT	450M
NUMBER OF FLOORS	100
FLOOR AREA	200,000M²
STRUCTURE	TECHNIKER
ENVIRONMENTAL	BDSP
STATUS	RESEARCH PROJECT

180 HAUER–KING HOUSE 1992

The completion in 1994 of this four-storey house on the end of a North London terrace was an important moment for Future Systems. 'It proved that we could build successfully and provide a service,' says Kaplicky. The narrow, shaded site in a conservation area posed a practical and planning challenge. Future Systems' bold solution draws on the lineage of the heavily glazed Modernist house (Pierre Chareau's Maison de Verre and houses by Paul Rudolph and Denys Lasdun are references) but adapted to the particularities of the site.

'We sorted out the classic problem of the London house by running the stair across the front,' explains Kaplicky. In this way the architects avoided the narrow spaces created when the stair runs front to back. Instead the living spaces are stacked up at the rear of the house across the full 6 metre width. The north-facing street facade is constructed of glass blocks, while the south-facing elevation comprises a sloping planar-glazed facade shaded by mature trees.

Inside, the light-filled spaces include a large kitchen and family room on the ground floor which is open to a galleried sitting room above. The floors span between blockwork walls, their undersides curving up where they meet the planar glazed facade to give an uplifting, airy feel. The bathrooms for the house (like those in

a slot

house in

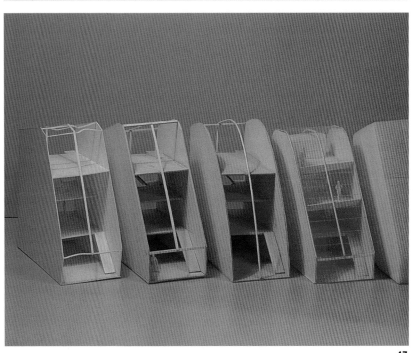

north elevation

south elevation

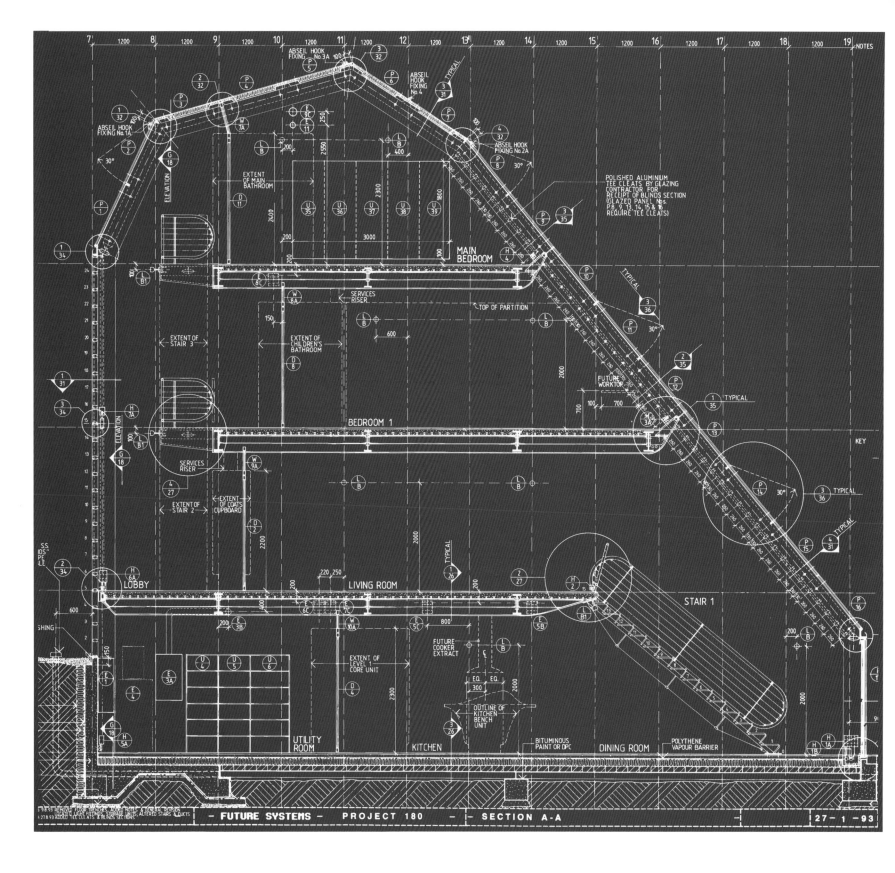

Project 222, see p102) were prefabricated and delivered as completed pods, saving a significant amount of time and money. The freestanding kitchen unit was custom-designed and made in aluminium, an application which the architects claim is a first.

Although this house is a one-off for which sixty drawings were required, Levete and Kaplicky think it still offers some lessons for low-cost, mass-produced housing. 'The materials are irrelevant,' they state. 'Architects use spaces in a way developers don't understand. This house shows how you can have open-plan space and lots of daylight despite the traditional problems of verticality in terraces.'

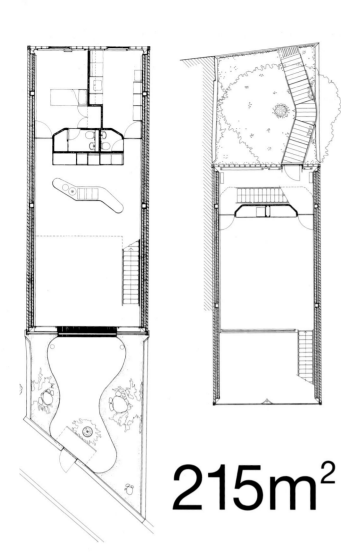

215m²

FAMILY HOUSE • STEEL SKELETON AND
FLOORS • BLOCKWORK PARTY WALLS •
GLASS AND GLASS BLOCK WALLS •
4 PREFABRICATED BATHROOM PODS

LENGTH	14.2M
WIDTH	6M
HEIGHT	14.2M
FLOOR AREA	215M²
STRUCTURE	ANTHONY HUNT ASSOCIATES
ENVIRONMENTAL	OVE ARUP & PARTNERS
CONSTRUCTION	JOHN SISK & SON

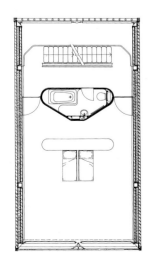

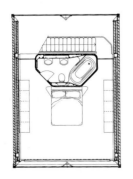

aluminium

white

yellow

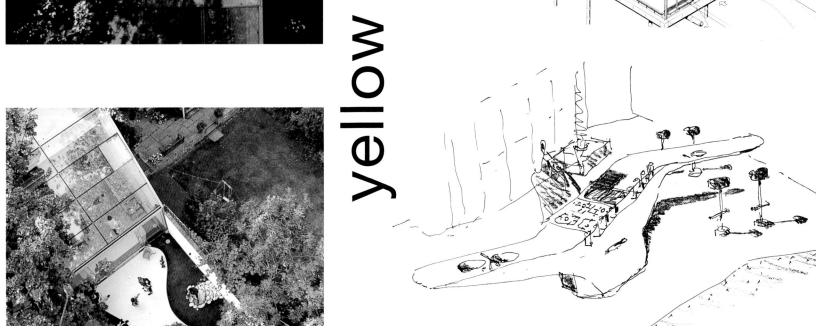

191 21ST CENTURY GALLERY 1993

Future Systems' speculative proposal for a new cultural building on the site of the old Bankside Power Station in London (now converted as the new Tate Gallery of Modern Art) shows a development of earlier projects, including the 1990 competition entry for the Museum of the Acropolis in Athens (see p193) and the 1992 scheme for a visitors' centre at Stonehenge (see p197).

The ambition of the project, which was developed in collaboration with the engineer Ove Arup and Partners, is to provide large, flexible areas of day-lit gallery space below a single-span glazed roof. Even before the current proposals to link the Tate with St Paul's, Future Systems perceived this scheme as directly linked to the cathedral via a new bridge and walkway. The main entrance to the gallery leads from this bridge on the river to the front of the building (as opposed to the current situation where the new Tate Gallery is entered from the street at the rear).

Inside the building a series of terraced galleries are connected by sweeping staircases. A custom-designed display system allows curators the freedom to create intimate areas or to keep the galleries open-plan for larger works, installations or performance art. The areas beneath the terraces house an auditorium and storage spaces. There is also a basement carpark and two floors of offices and a delivery area integrated into the smooth form of the building at the rear.

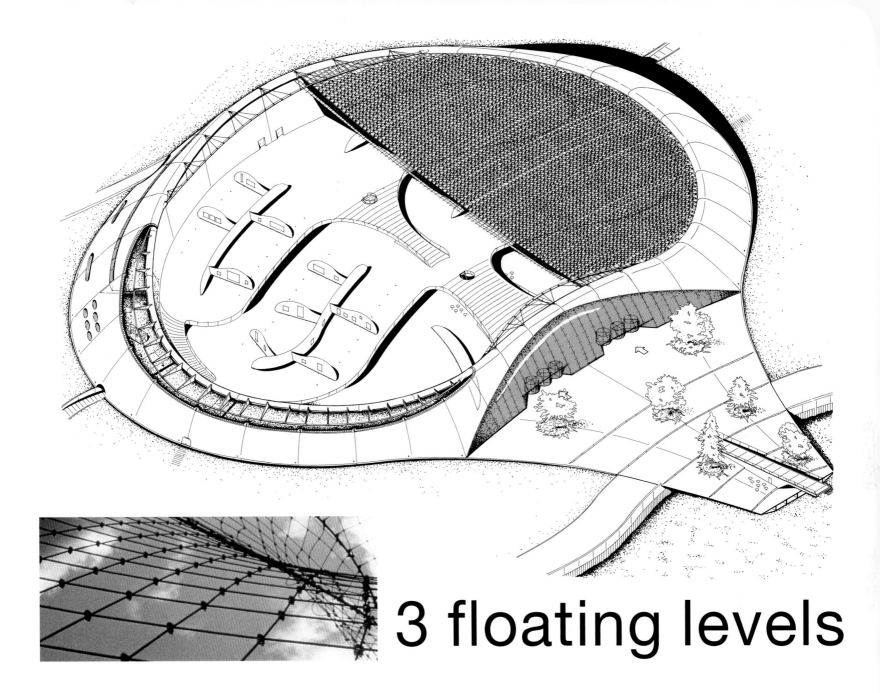

3 floating levels

Among the most innovative features of this scheme is its highly engineered 'smart' roof. This is formed from a double net of tension cables spanning the roof from a perimeter beam. Mounted on these cables are hundreds of shell-like canopies which allow only north light to enter. This light passes into the canopy and is then directed deep into the space via a series of internal reflectors. Integrated into the roof framework are a number of other functions, including solar cells, ventilation ducts and lighting tracks. Other air-handling services are contained in the floor voids.

The smooth, organically shaped form of this scheme is a good example of Future Systems' drive to challenge the conventional orthogonal shape of buildings. Kaplicky feels that 'spaces defined by eight corners are not compulsory or necessary'. The aluminium shell, with its colourful spray-painted finish, also challenges the dominance of brick and concrete construction.

Although the management and trustees at the Tate Gallery could have constructed a new building for a lower cost than converting Bankside Power Station, they chose the latter option for their new museum of modern art. Future commentators are bound to question the wisdom of this decision. Meanwhile the research carried out for the roof proposal for this gallery has not been wasted: the same technology is now being applied in the architects' scheme for the Ark (see p110).

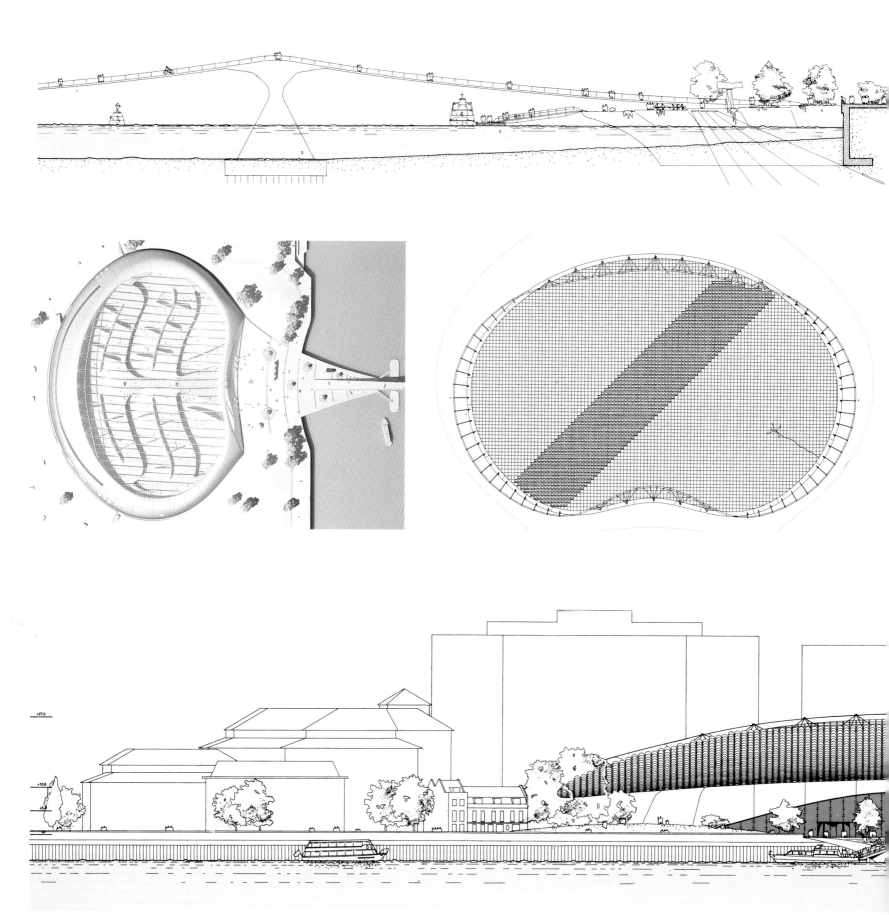

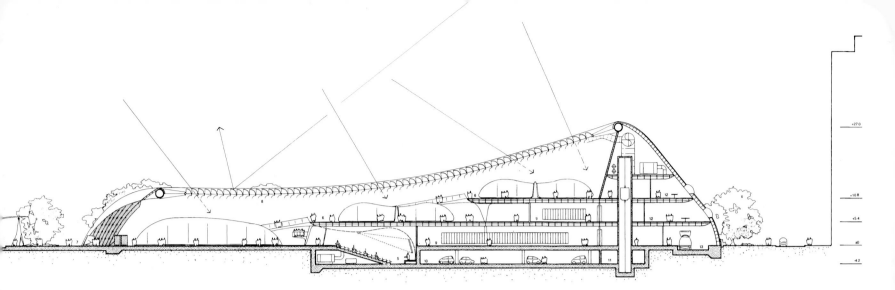

ribbon bridge

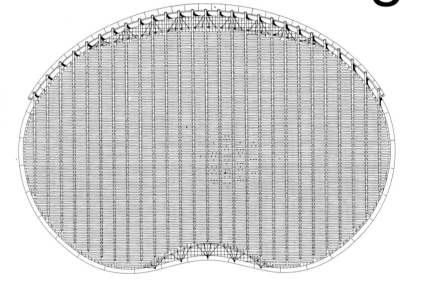

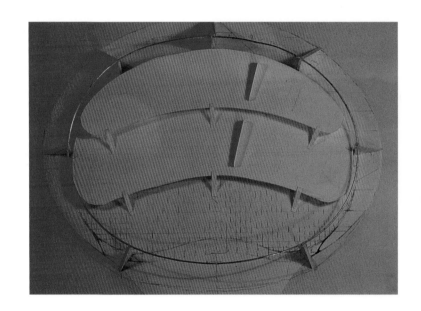

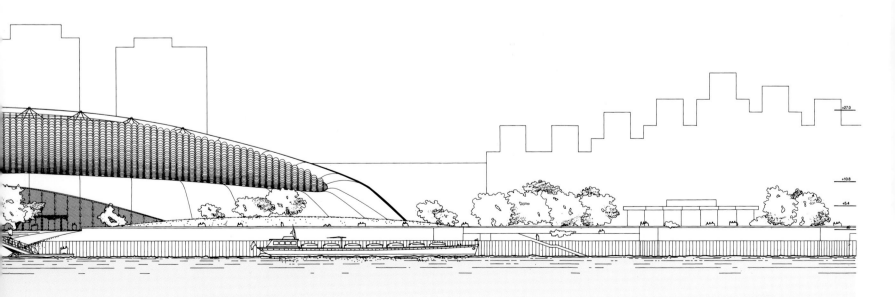

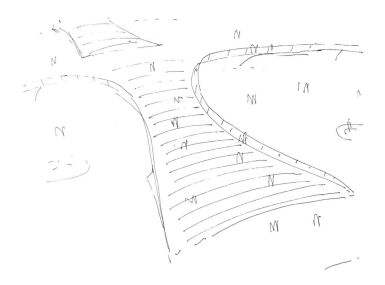

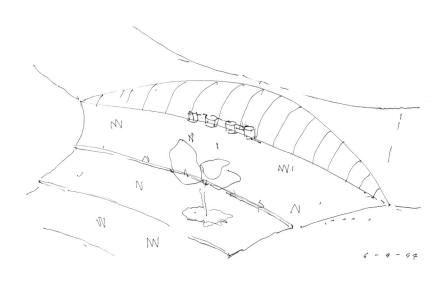

6 - 9 - 97

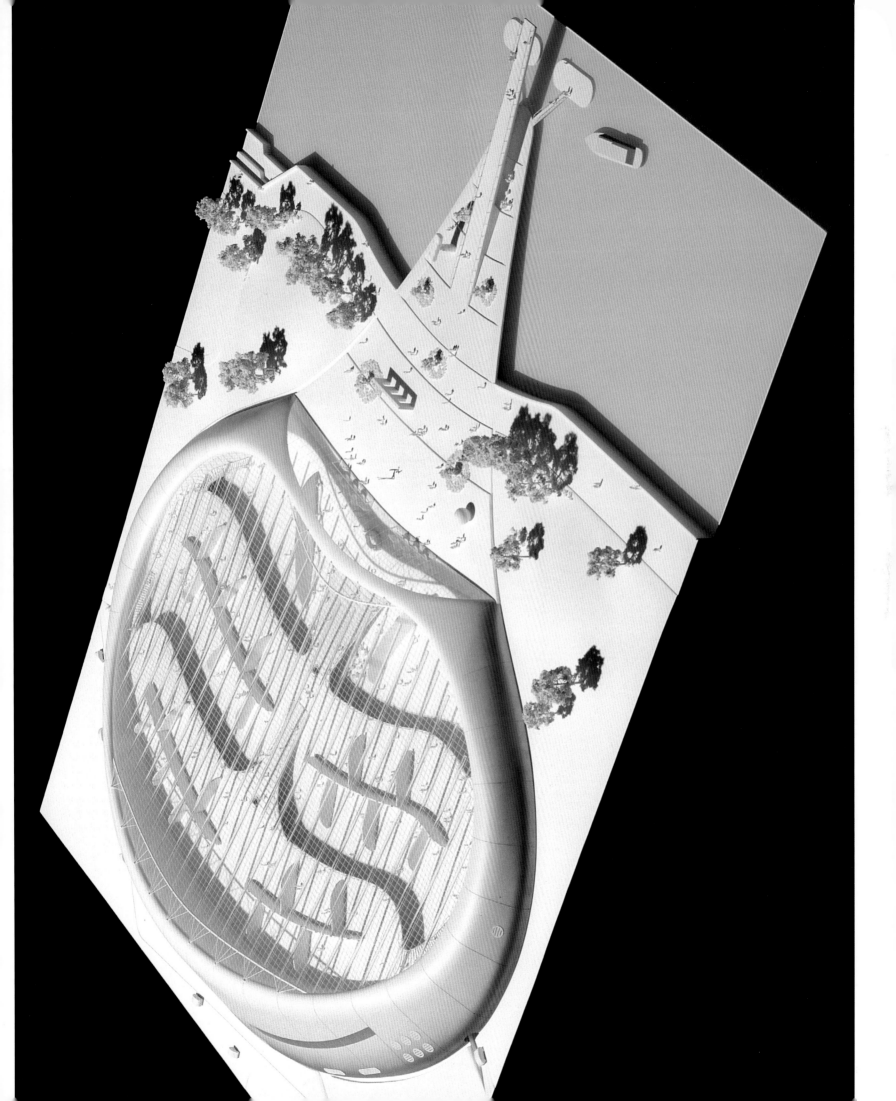

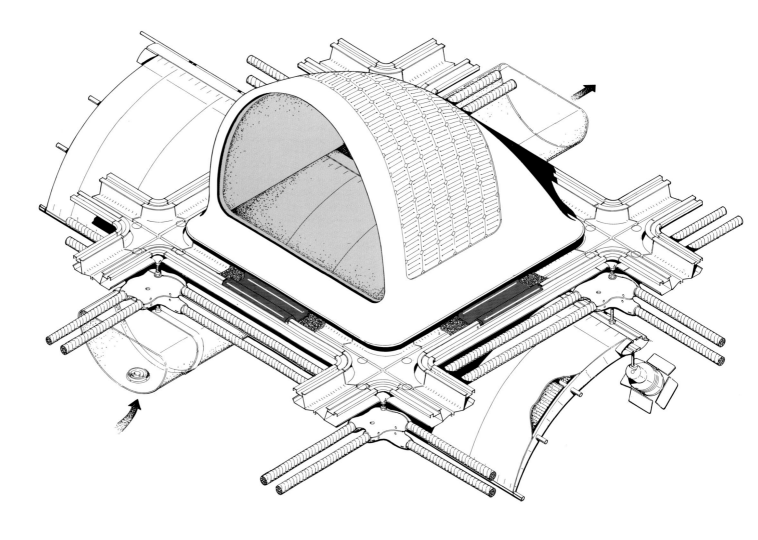

suspended roof
light penetration

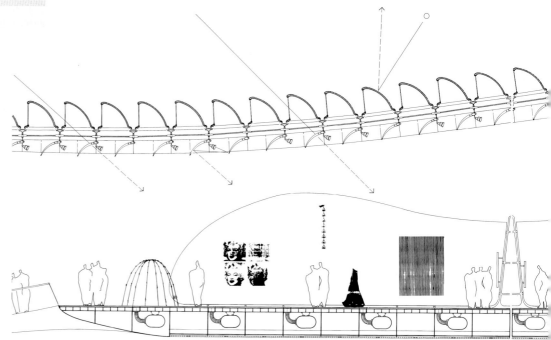

GALLERY BUILDING • 3 EXHIBITION LEVELS •
CABLE ROOF • STEEL STRUCTURE • NATURAL LIGHT
• SHELL ROOF SYSTEM • SOLAR CELLS • SCULPTURE
GARDEN • RIBBON BRIDGE ENTRANCE

WIDTH	96M
HEIGHT	27M
FLOOR AREA	7,500M²
STRUCTURE	OVE ARUP & PARTNERS
ENVIRONMENTAL	OVE ARUP & PARTNERS
STATUS	RESEARCH PROJECT

north light only

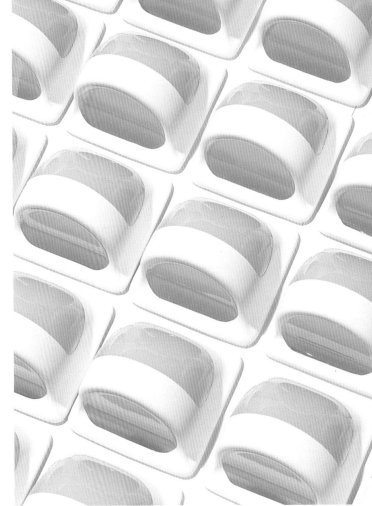

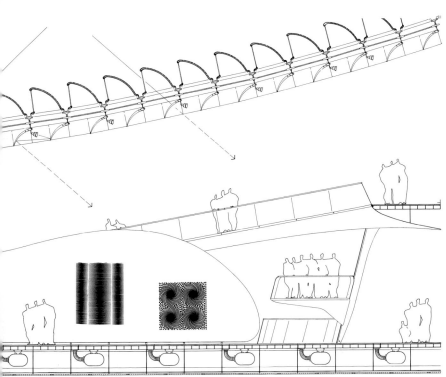

JOSEF'S BED

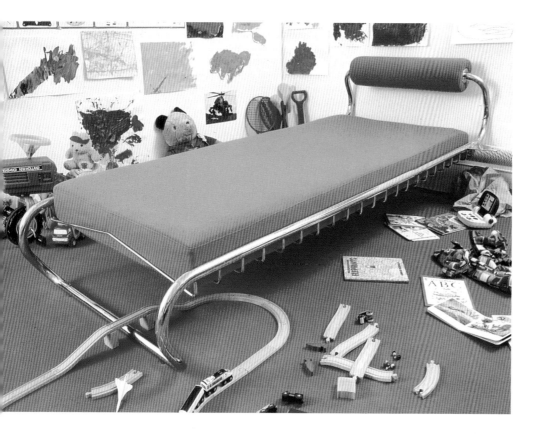

This elegant and lightweight bed has a foot at one end and is supported from a wall at the other. Its tubular metal structure draws on the innovative furniture in the same material designed by early pioneers such as Mies van der Rohe, Marcel Breuer and Mart Stam in the 1920s.

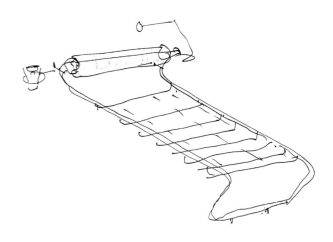

This oval wardrobe is a response to a private commission for a place to store clothes. Its compact form is designed with drawers at either end and doors on both sides, allowing a couple to keep their clothes separately. A perforated aluminium skin surrounds the central hanging structure and the whole is raised up on castors for mobility. 'People still think of it as "high-tech",' says Kaplicky, who points out that rather than being 'futuristic', many of the inspirations for this piece lie in the 1930s furniture of Mies, Breuer and Pierre Chareau.

ANNE'S CUPBOARD

FURNITURE

The design for this easy chair is an attempt to challenge the conventional form of the armchair with something more comfortable and compact. Two simple pads are linked by a strong stainless steel connection which lends a spring to the back. The chair is fitted with four castors so it can be moved easily around the home.

'When architects draw the plan of a house they always put in one Le Corbusier sofa and two armchairs,' explains Kaplicky, who designed this seating/sleeping system as an alternative solution. Fixed in the centre of the architect's own living space, it functions as a kind of giant foam 'dinghy' as users take off their shoes and jump in. It can accommodate up to eight people in the minimum possible area. The ply and foam construction provides comfortable seating for people watching television or talking together. It also makes an ideal play area for children or adults and the perfect place for guests to sleep.

DINGHY

ALUMINIUM TABLE

Now the dining table of Kaplicky and Levete, this is intended as the prototype for an affordable, mass-produced piece. The self-finished surface is cut from honeycomb aluminium sheet and raised up on a structure of stainless-steel rods on castors.

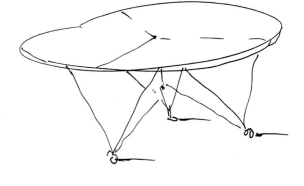

The top of this meeting table, designed for the Future Systems office, is of laminated ply construction. Kaplicky explains its likeness to an old-fashioned aeroplane propeller: 'Architects often used to have them hanging on their office walls.' The curved-edge surface has been finished in a tactile, shiny black lacquer and is fixed to an aluminium base.

WOODEN TABLE

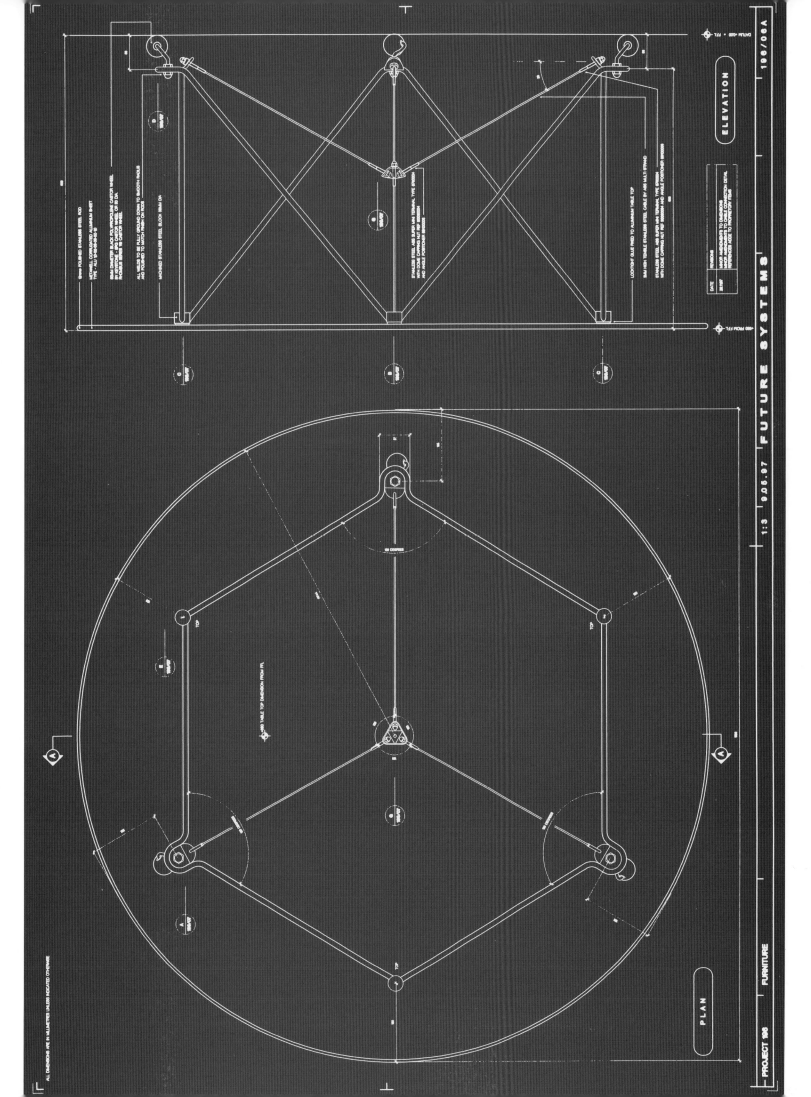

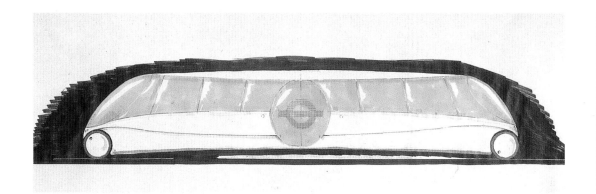

Jan Kaplicky travels regularly by bus in London and the Superbus is his personal response to many years of uncomfortable and noisy journeys. He thinks it is incredible that 'you see old people and women with children struggling up and down the stairs.' In contrast the Superbus is a streamlined single-deck vehicle which lowers at stops for easy access. It has a semi-monocoque aluminium shell, a capacity of 90 passengers and is electrically powered (recharging would take place at terminus points). Nearly four million passengers use London's 5,500 buses per day and the number is growing. Both the Government and London Transport agree that buses are the answer to the capital's traffic problems, but the existing vehicles are mostly old, uncomfortable, unreliable and environmentally unfriendly. Future Systems' Superbus could be the perfect solution.

203 SUPERBUS 1993

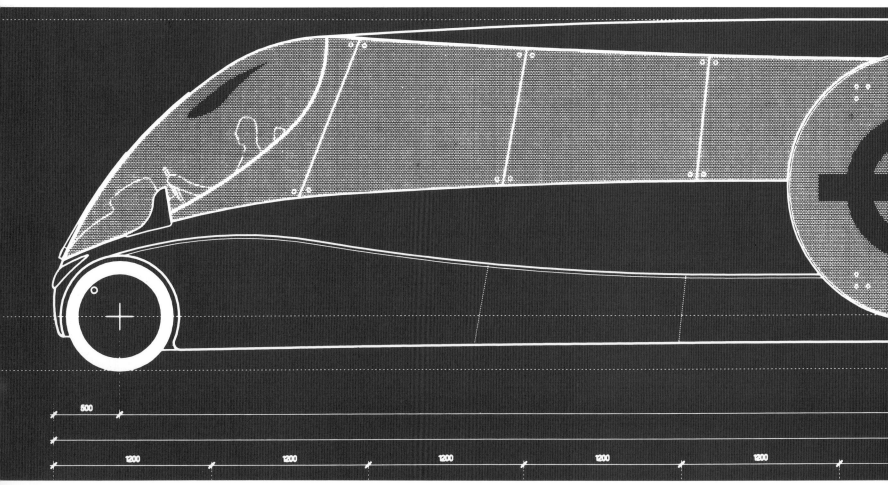

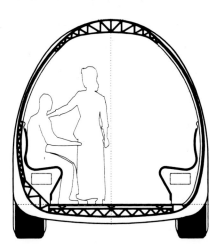

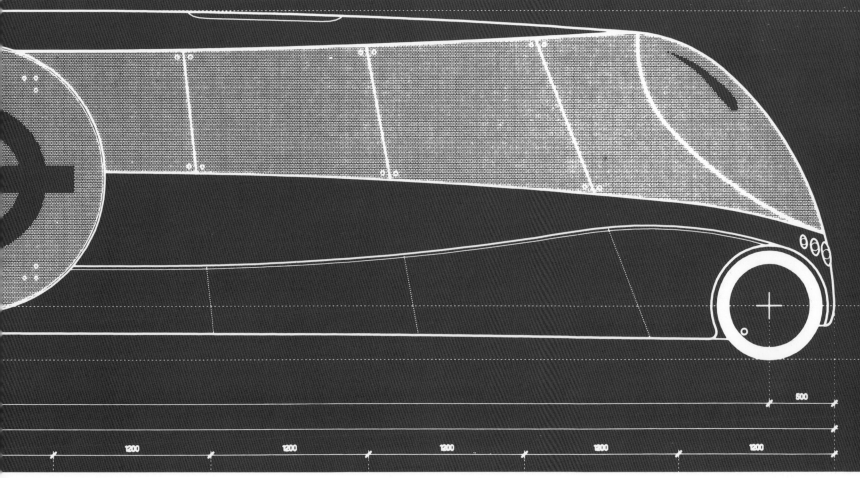

205 CROYDON BRIDGE   1993

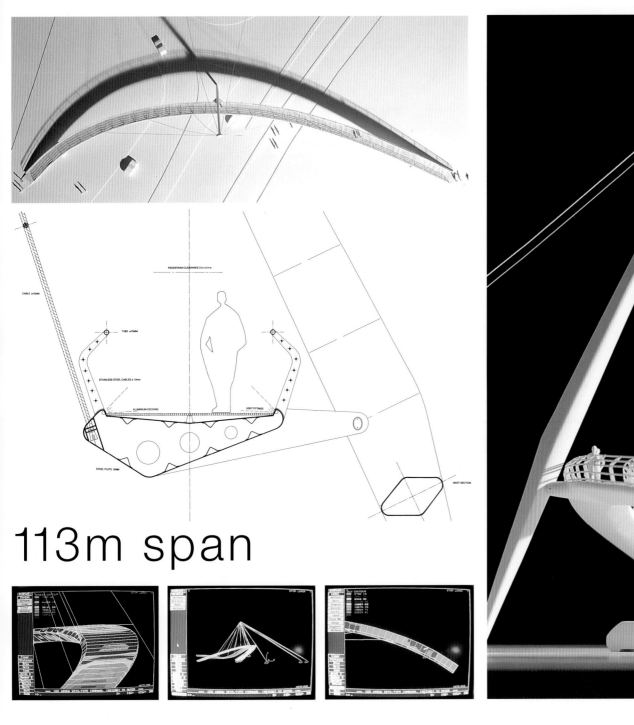

113m span

In 1993, as one of a number of architectural practices selected to propose improvements to the centre of Croydon, Future Systems was commissioned to design a new footbridge between the Fairfield Hall and the Queen's Garden. The architects' solution is an elegant arched bridge, which curves in plan around mature trees. The steel structure is supported at each end and from above by stainless-steel cables attached to a single inclined mast. The perforated aluminium deck rises in a series of shallow ramped steps, shortening the necessary span of the bridge and allowing disabled users and pushchairs to cross comfortably. As with many Future Systems projects, all the elements in this scheme are intended to be prefabricated for maximum quality and minimum disruption on site. Although this bridge remains unbuilt, elements of the concept, including the prefabrication, integral lighting and aluminium deck, have been realized in the completed scheme for the floating Docklands bridge (Project 219, see p84).

1948–89

10,000 dead

209 PRAGUE MEMORIAL 1995

During the years of the communist dictatorship in Czechoslovakia (1948–89) nearly 300 political prisoners were executed and some 10,000 people died in concentration camps. For twenty years Jan Kaplicky lived under this regime and remembers people who suffered and disappeared. As a way of honouring these victims and a nation of people whose human values were destroyed, Future Systems designed a memorial for Prague to link the Old Town and the castle by a new pedestrian route.

The site for the memorial on Letenska Plateau is symbolic. In 1955, two years after Stalin's death, a colossal 14,000-ton statue of the dictator (the largest likeness ever made) was erected here to watch over the city. The structure was demolished in 1962, but many people still remember it as a symbol of oppression.

Future Systems proposed a memorial on this site which would cut deep into the Plateau and be lined with black glass – a local material – engraved with the names of all those who died. To introduce a personal element to the project, the architects suggested that the sides of the memorial should contain small glazed showcases filled with everyday objects and mementos from the period. No stone – the favoured material of dictators – would be used. Instead, the forty-two steps across the memorial, marking forty-two years of oppression, are stainless steel.

Kaplicky sent this speculative scheme to a minister of the Czech Republic suggesting that the memorial be funded by selling properties illegally impounded by the Communist Party and by reclaiming money raised from the export of uranium mined by prisoners. He met with a curt rebuff and the memorial remains unbuilt.

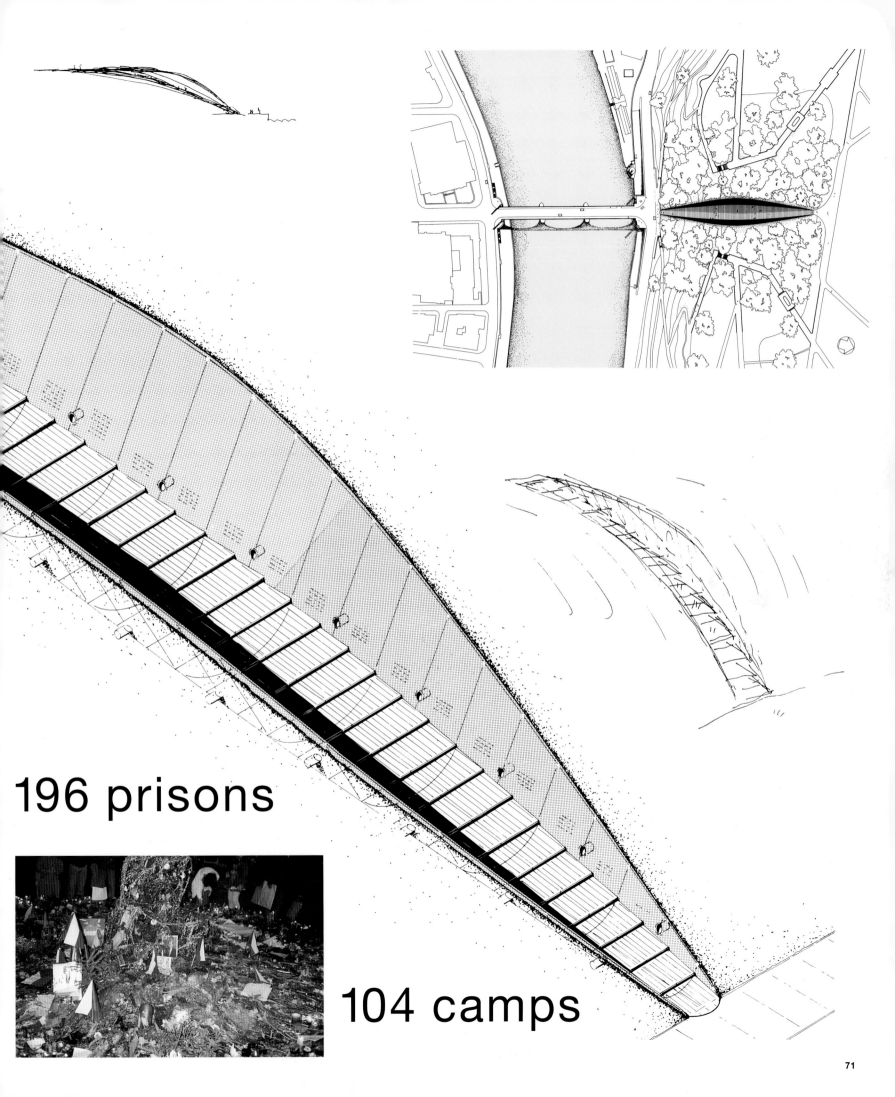

196 prisons

104 camps

MEMORIAL • IN-SITU STRUCTURE • BLACK GLASS
CLADDING • 42 STAINLESS-STEEL GRATING STEPS
• 26 DISPLAY CASES • INSCRIBED VICTIMS' NAMES

LENGTH	200M
WIDTH	35M
STRUCTURE	OVE ARUP & PARTNERS
STATUS	RESEARCH PROJECT

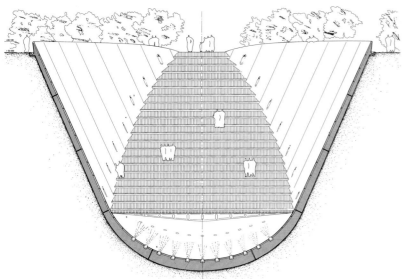

216 JOSEF K HOUSE 1997

Kaplicky is optimistic that this proposal, for the kind of home his son Josef might have when he grows up, will seem normal in thirty years time. The scheme is designed for a rural or semi-rural setting where it would be cut into the ground to make a striking, but not overpowering, impact.

Like the Media Centre at Lord's, the house has a semi-monocoque aluminium structure which allows its curvaceous form and colourful spray-painted finish. Glazed openings in the shell provide top lighting and views out over the landscape. Inside, the open-plan living and sleeping areas are defined not by partitions but by an undulating, sculpted floor. The bathrooms are delivered to the site as prefabricated pods, a method already used by Future Systems at the Hauer–King House and the house in Wales. Other elements of the project, including the oval bed, sofa system and kitchen unit, have also been tested in previously built work. Although futuristic looking, this house is not an unrealizable vision, but something which could be built now. It also illustrates Future Systems' interests in alternative models for housing. With little adaption, this scheme could provide an economic, energy-efficient, flexible and easily produced solution to today's housing needs.

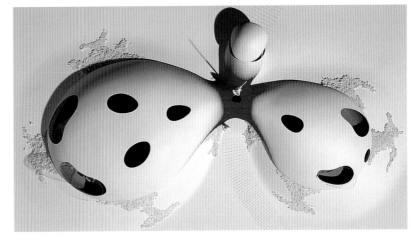

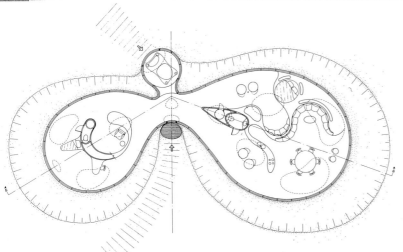

FAMILY HOUSE • SEMI-MONOCOQUE LIGHTWEIGHT
ALUMINIUM ROOFING • RETAINING WALLS •
SLOPING FLOOR • INTEGRATED CARPORT

LENGTH	31.2M
WIDTH	13.2M
HEIGHT	4.8M
FLOOR AREA	150M²
STRUCTURE	OVE ARUP & PARTNERS
ENVIRONMENTAL	OVE ARUP & PARTNERS
STATUS	RESEARCH PROJECT

undulating floor   monocoque roof

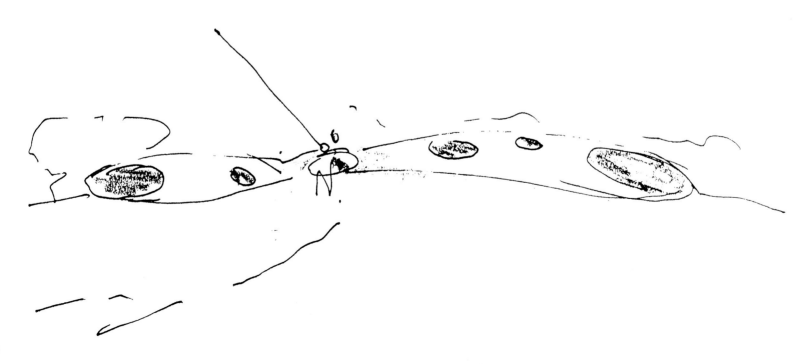

217 YOKOHAMA PORT TERMINAL

1996

with the Richard Rogers Partnership

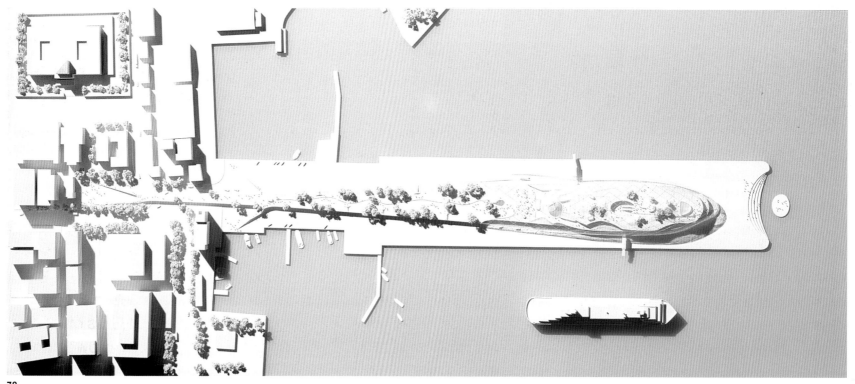

PORT TERMINAL BUILDING • STEEL AND GLASS
DIAGONAL GRID • 3 LEVELS • DOUBLE-SKIN
SHELL STRUCTURE • PARK CONNECTION TO
TOWN CENTRE

HEIGHT	32M
LENGTH	460M
FLOOR AREA	46,000M²
STRUCTURE	OVE ARUP & PARTNERS
ENVIRONMENTAL	OVER ARUP & PARTNERS
STATUS	COMPETITION ENTRY

This competition entry for a new ferry terminal in Yokohama, Japan, alludes to the sinuous forms of marine life and the structure of ships. 'It's basically an upside-down hull,' explains Kaplicky. To draw people in, the terminal has a 'tongue' which forms a route into the city centre. 'We wanted it to be a place to visit for the view,' continues the architect, 'so it always has life in it, not just when a boat comes in or leaves.' Visitors walk up the route and through an internal garden to a glazed viewing 'blob' at the end. The business of loading and unloading ships takes place on a lower level, providing a bustling spectacle for the gathered crowd above.

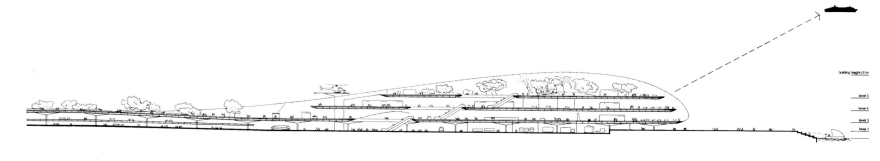

continuous

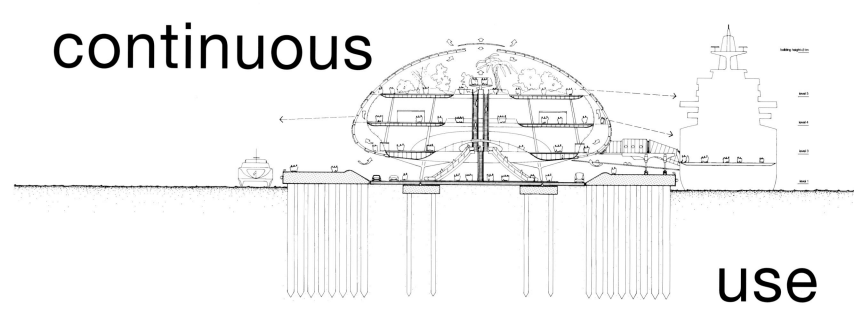

use

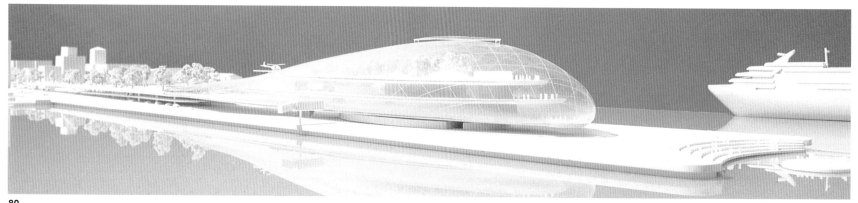

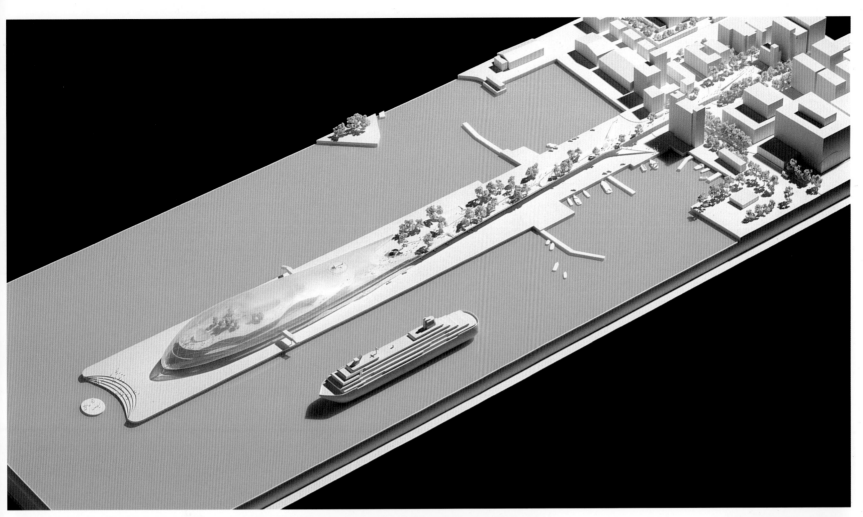

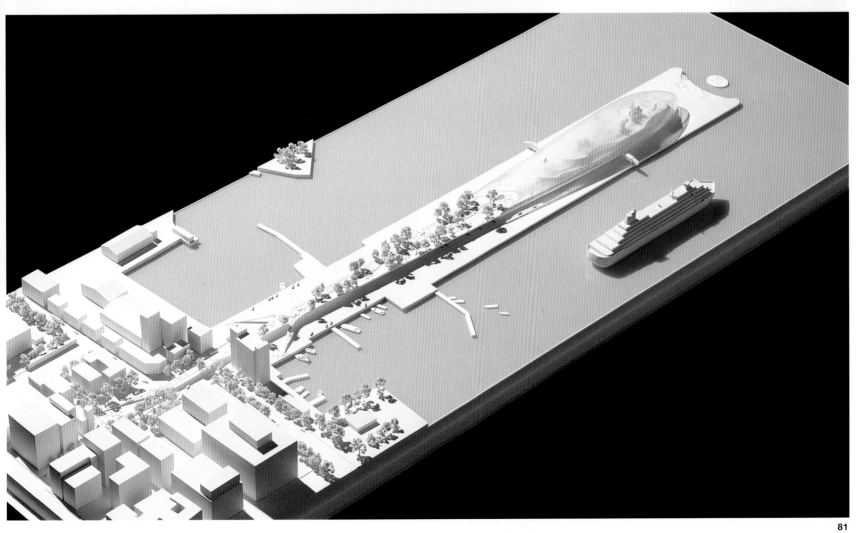

216 TATE GALLERY OF MODERN ART 1994

Soon after Future Systems completed its speculative scheme for a new gallery on the site of Bankside Power Station (see p54), the Tate Gallery launched a competition to design a new museum of modern art in the shell of the defunct building. Future Systems' entry proposed a vast glazed roof to be slung over the husk of Bankside, extending out towards the Thames to enclose shops, restaurants and foyer space on a series of new terraces. At the rear the roof curves down to create areas for services and deliveries. Inside the old turbine hall a new set of galleries are stacked up as discrete spaces for displaying works, each with controlled top-lighting. The scheme incorporates many ideas from Project 191, notably the cable-net roof and footbridge, but the judges eventually selected a scheme which proposed subtle embellishment over radical representation. The competition provided an opportunity to explore ideas which were later developed for the Ark (see p110).

new wrap

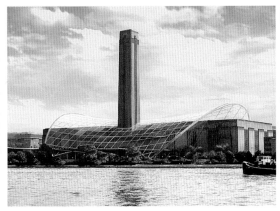

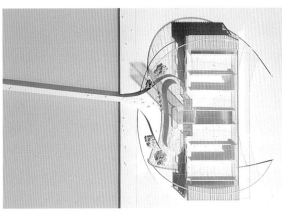

219 DOCKLANDS BRIDGE 1996

Finished only two years after the Hauer–King House, this imaginatively conceived floating footbridge in the Docklands area of London attracted a great deal of publicity when it was completed. It also confirmed Future Systems' ability to build its innovative projects.

The bridge, which won a competition commissioned by the London Docklands Development Corporation, spans 94 metres across West India Quay with Canary Wharf on one side and a row of early nineteenth-century warehouses on the other. Ancient arched bridges, rope bridges and pontoon structures are among the references for the project. More characteristic of the diverse origins of the architects' ideas, though, is the acknowledged influence of brightly coloured water insects and the dramatic cut of high fashion clothes.

For Future Systems, the potential for prefabrication has always been an important consideration. The ideal, as espoused by many Modern Movement architects, is that work created in a dry, efficient environment can be more economic, controlled and highly finished than work which is subject to the conditions of the site and weather outside. The concept of the bridge as a floating structure, lowered onto the water after completion, allowed all fabrication to take place in such controlled conditions.

In form the bridge comprises a mild steel structure with an aluminium deck, the whole resting on four pairs of pontoons which are themselves attached to concrete piles. The two sides of the bridge gently ramp up to a middle section which opens hydraulically to allow boats to pass through. Lighting for this bridge is central to the concept. Integral units in the handrails illuminate the walkway at night, with additional runway lighting in the deck delineating the elegant tapering plan.

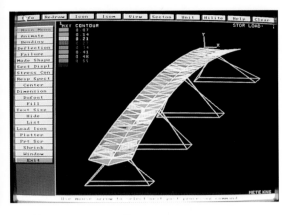

design

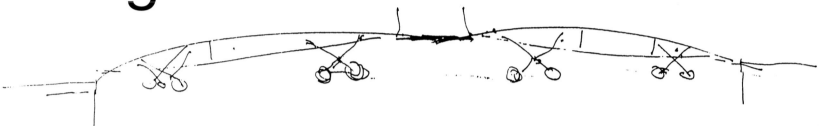

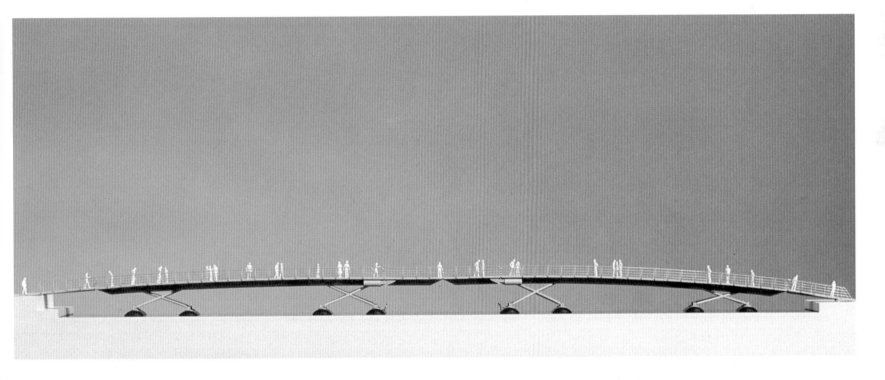

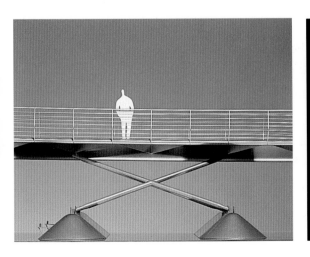
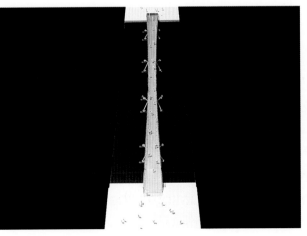
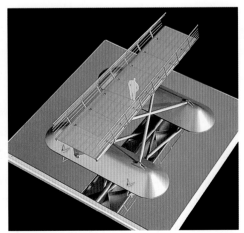

For Kaplicky one of the greatest moments in the process of making the bridge was its transportation in two halves on a lorry (with a police escort) from the workshop to the site – an event which confirmed his belief in the possibilities of prefabrication. For the young project architect Angus Pond, now an associate at Future Systems, the bridge marks an early and successful collaboration. For local people and visitors to Docklands meanwhile, this link provides both a practical and exhilarating way to cross the quay as the floating structure moves gently beneath them.

PONTOON BRIDGE • CENTRAL HYDRAULICALLY OPERATED OPENING • PREFABRICATED TUBULAR STEEL STRUCTURE • ALUMINIUM DECKING • 3 LIGHTING SYSTEMS • 4 GUIDANCE PILES

SPAN	80M
MAX WIDTH	5.4M
STRUCTURE	ANTHONY HUNT ASSOCIATES
QUANTITY SURVEYOR	BUCKNALL AUSTIN
LIGHTING	LIGHTING DESIGN PARTNERSHIP
CONSTRUCTION	LITTLEHAMPTON WELDING

construction   transport

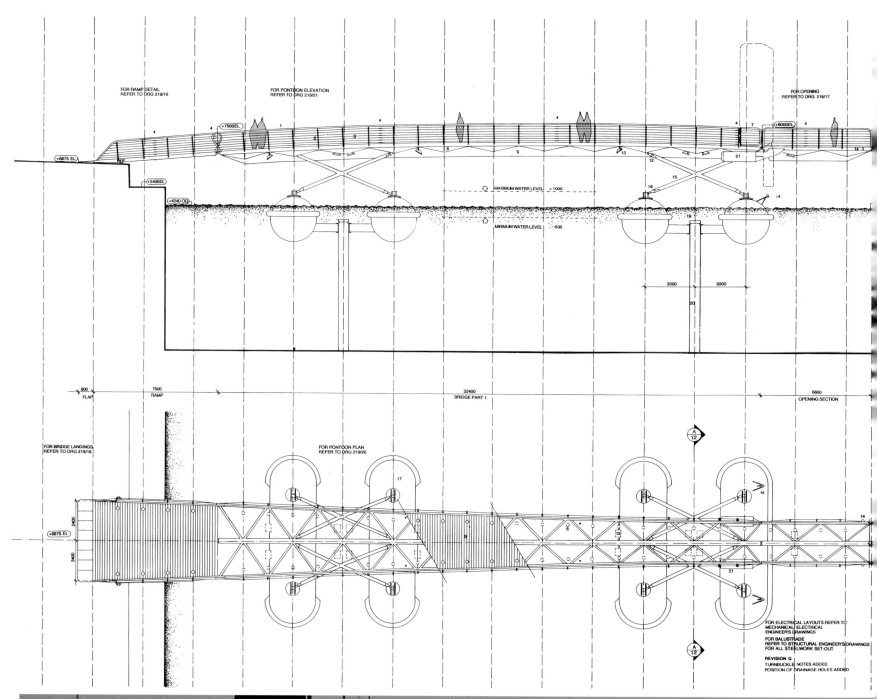

FOR RAMP DETAIL
REFER TO DRG 219/16

FOR PONTOON ELEVATION
REFER TO DRG 219/21

FOR OPENING
REFER TO DRG. 219/17

+7500EL

+8000EL

+6875 EL

+5400EL

+4240 CXD

MAXIMUM WATER LEVEL + 1000

MINIMUM WATER LEVEL - 600

3000   3000

900   7500   32400   6600
FLAP   RAMP   BRIDGE PART 1   OPENING SECTION

FOR BRIDGE LANDINGS
REFER TO DRG.219/18

FOR PONTOON PLAN
REFER TO DRG.219/20

+6875 EL   2400

2400

FOR ELECTRICAL LAYOUTS REFER TO
MECHANICAL ELECTRICAL
ENGINEER'S DRAWINGS

FOR BALUSTRADE
REFER TO STRUCTURAL ENGINEER'S DRAWINGS
FOR ALL STEELWORK SET-OUT.

REVISION G
TURNBUCKLE NOTES ADDED
POSITION OF DRAINAGE HOLES ADDED

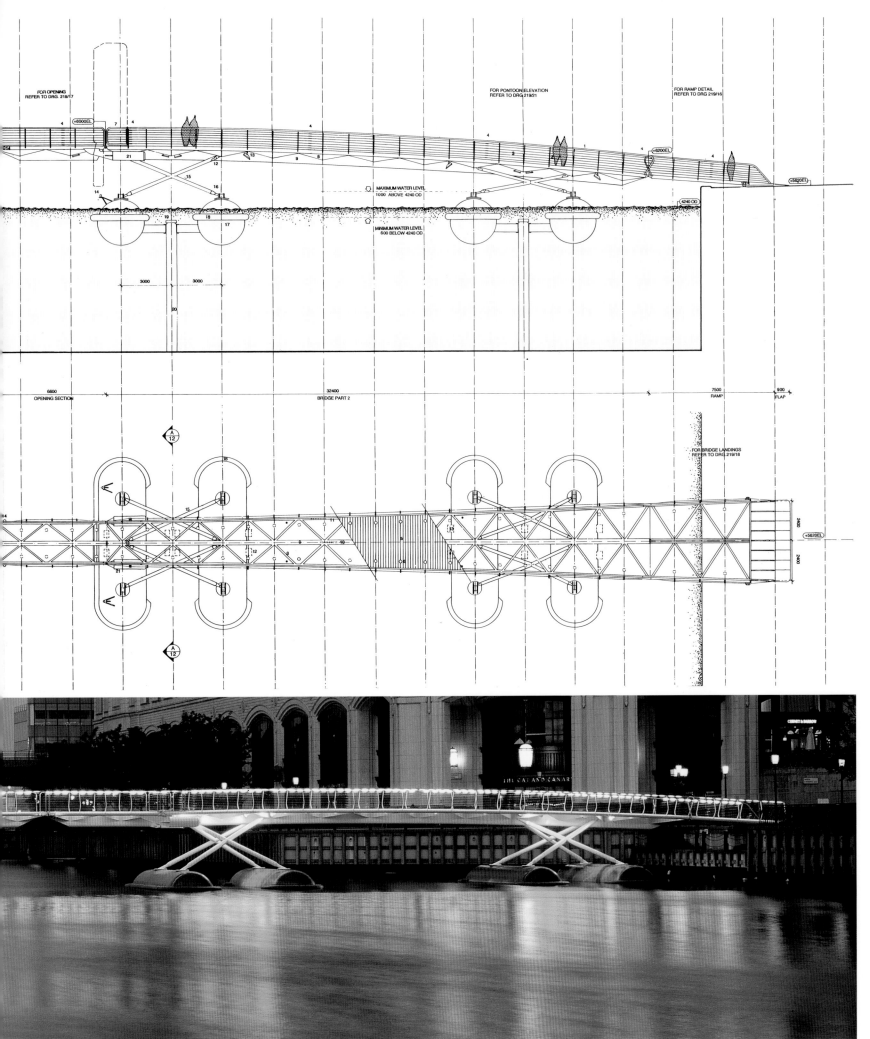

FOR OPENING
REFER TO DRG. 219/17

+8000EL

7

4

4

21

12

13

9

8

3

1

FOR PONTOON ELEVATION
REFER TO DRG 219/21

4

4

4

+6200EL

4

FOR RAMP DETAIL
REFER TO DRG 219/16

+5620EL

15

16

14

MAXIMUM WATER LEVEL
1000 ABOVE 4240 OD

4240 OD

19

18

17

MINIMUM WATER LEVEL
600 BELOW 4240 OD

3000

3000

20

6600

OPENING SECTION

32400

BRIDGE PART 2

7500

RAMP

900

FLAP

A
12

18

FOR BRIDGE LANDINGS
REFER TO DRG 219/18

15

13

2400

+5620EL

12

8

10

5

21

2400

A
12

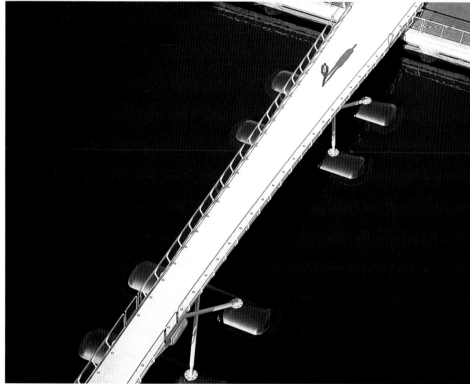

light

colour

221 LORD'S MEDIA CENTRE 1994

The completion in spring 1999 of the NatWest Media Centre at Lord's Cricket Ground in London represents a landmark in the work of Future Systems as well as in the history of architecture. The practice was invited, along with other leading architects, to submit ideas for the new building in late 1994.

'We decided to go for broke,' explains Levete of their bold scheme. What the architects proposed was to create a new kind of building, one which would not compete with the famous structures which line the perimeter of the cricket ground. Taking the function and site of the building as their starting point, Future Systems drew further inspiration from the form of the camera (after all, the building is about framing the views of commentators) and the high-tech protective clothing of athletes. The result was an inspiring proposal for a streamlined aluminium pod raised nearly 14 metres above the ground. Not only did the scheme offer the excellent sightlines and facilities that commentators need, but it would be constructed unlike any other building.

The Marylebone Cricket Club selected Future Systems' proposal as the winner in late 1995. The dramatic image released to the media astounded the public and made the front page of *The Times* where Jack Bailey, the former secretary of the club, was quoted as saying: 'The media centre is proof of the exciting, cultural change on the face of Lord's.' Meanwhile Jonathan Glancey, the architecture critic of the *Independent*, hailed it as 'one of the most original and elegant buildings in Britain.'

Having proved that a conventionally clad structure was not the best option for the building, Future Systems pursued their plan of fabricating the pod as a semi-monocoque aluminium structure in a boatyard. A number of advantages determined this approach. Among the most significant of these is the fact that aluminium will not corrode, can be recycled (the material used for the building is itself 80 per cent recycled), and can be formed to make a waterproof skin which is also structural thus obviating the need for a frame or cladding.

The shell, made up of computer-cut 6mm and 12mm aluminium sheets with ribs and spars, was pre-assembled in the Pendennis boatyard for checking and then divided into 26 three-metre widths and transported to site on the back of a lorry. The 40-metre-wide pod was then bolted and welded together on two giant concrete legs (these support the structure as well as housing lifts and escape stairs). On the exterior the weld lines of the building have been filled and the whole thing sanded down and spray-painted to a smooth seamless finish. Expansion joints, usually incorporated in buildings to allow the structure to move, are not necessary here. Instead the building moves as a united whole. A single gutter is recessed into the structure, collecting water and draining it through internal pipes.

A vast wall of laminated toughened glass overlooks the cricket ground on the west front of the pod. This highly engineered glazing is inclined at 25 degrees to prevent reflections onto the pitch. Only one opening is made in the glass: a window for the Test Match special studio allows the sound of play and applause to enter the box.

Although the structure of the building is impressive, the experience of being inside is just as significant for the architects. 'I don't want it to be seen just as a technical achievement,' says Kaplicky. 'I want it to be considered a spatial achievement too.' While most conventional buildings have floors, walls and ceilings and thus eight corners, the Media Centre has curved ends like an aeroplane or a boat. The connection of the

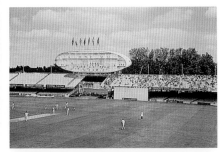

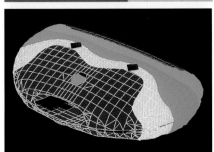

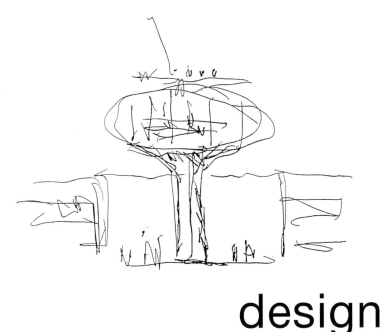

design

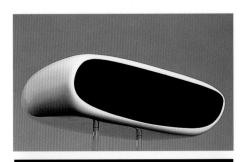

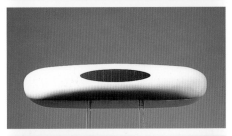

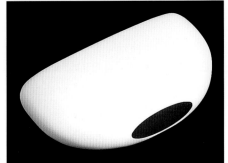

SEMI-MONOCOQUE ALUMINIUM
PRESS BOX • FIRE PROTECTION
•SUSPENDED MEZZANINE FLOOR
•SOFT LINING • CAPACITY: 120
WRITERS, 100 BROADCASTERS•
50-SEAT RESTAURANT

WIDTH	40M
DEPTH	20M
HEIGHT	21M
FLOOR AREA	600M²

STRUCTURE
      OVE ARUP & PARTNERS
ENVIRONMENT BÜRO HAPPOLD
GLAZING
 BILLINGS DESIGN ASSOCIATES
CONSTRUCTION
      PENDENNIS SHIPYARD

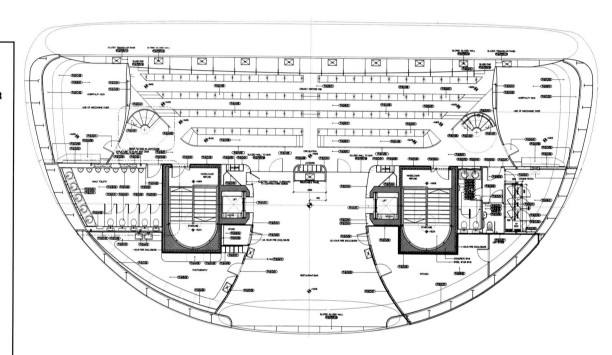

manufacturing

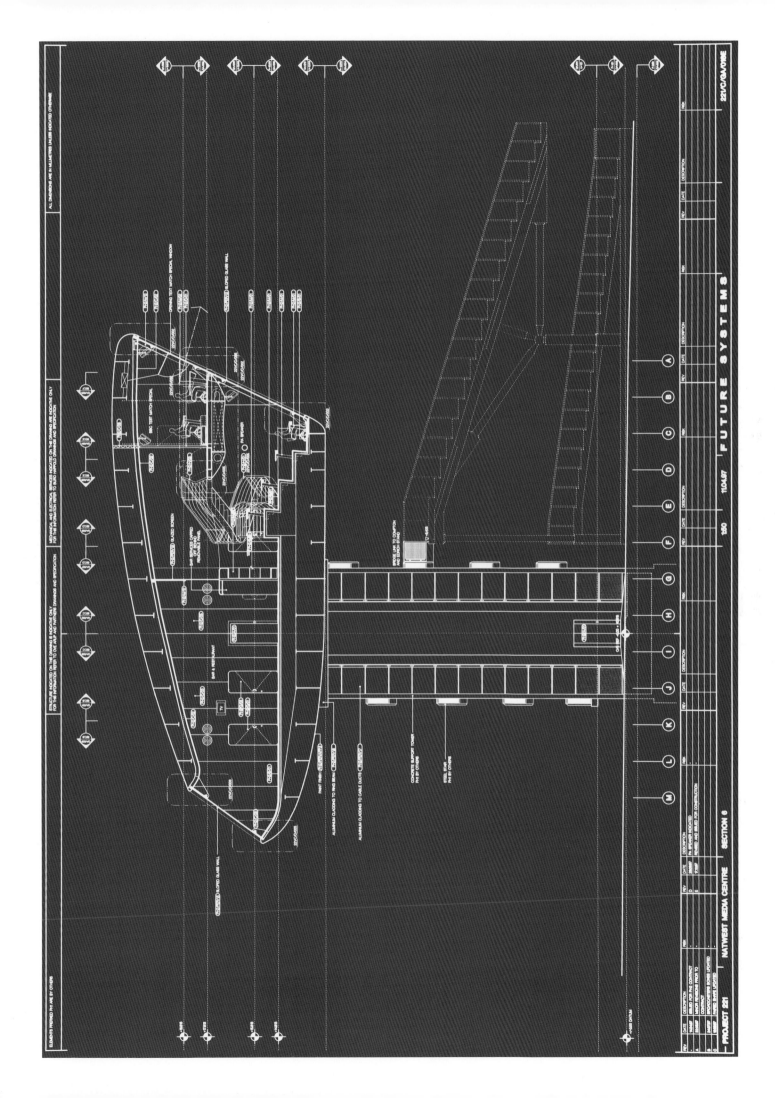

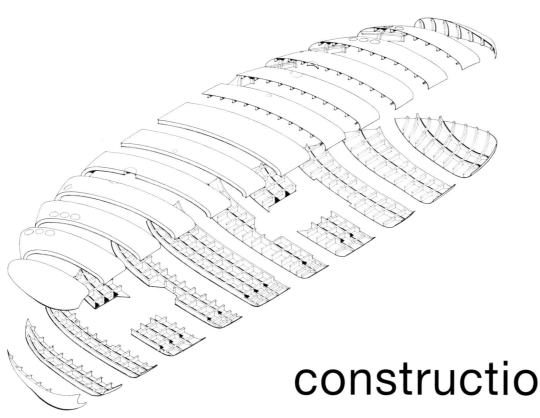

construction sequence

26 elements
3 x 20m size
4t-6t weight

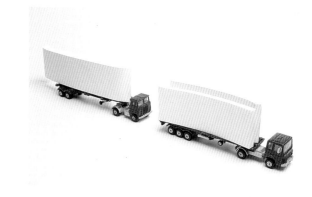

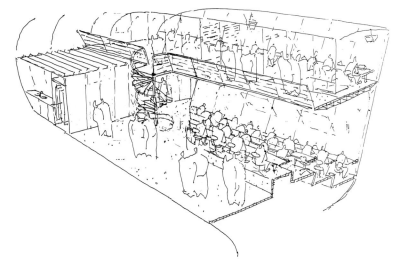

colour

building to these industrially manufactured products is further enforced by the use of carpet curving up the sides and the soft finishes on the ceiling (an effect the architects refer to as 'Blue Suede Shoes').

The facilities provided in this building are manifold. Two hundred and fifty journalists and photographers, from print, radio and television, are given the best view of the game. One hundred and twenty journalists sit on chairs arranged in four tiers along the main glazed front. Each is provided with power and a bank of phone lines, as well as a personal supply of cool air (just like in a car or plane). Individual broadcast studios are arranged above along a mezzanine floor which is suspended from the top of the pod. Beneath raised floor and wall panels is concealed a whole gamut of cables and ducts for the supply of power, information

technology and air handling. The building also houses some of London's most spectacular hospitality areas. A fifty-seat restaurant and bar has views out over tree tops to the east, while two suites located at either end of the pod offer guests enviable views out over the ground.

In the lineage of modern architecture, the Media Centre sets an important precedent. It shows how a building of high-quality both in terms of construction and spatial experience can be made using materials and processes which could be adapted to mass production. It is something that many architects have pursued but rarely realized. But, as critic Colin Davies has written in the *Architects' Journal*, the Media Centre is 'unquestionably the real thing'.

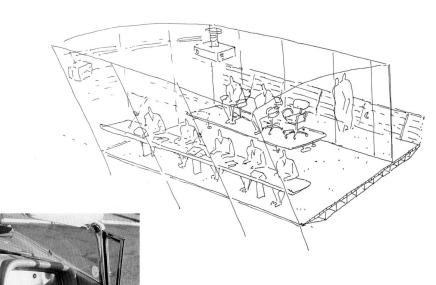

softness

details

222 HOUSE IN WALES 1994

In December 1998, a media storm broke over a small private house recently completed on the Pembrokeshire coast of Wales. Newspapers clamoured over the story of the building, its owners and architects, and people stared in amazement at the pictures on the pages. This was no ordinary house, but another extraordinary project from the office of Future Systems.

Commissioned by the Labour MP Bob Marshall-Andrews and his wife Gill, the new house replaces a timber holiday home converted from an old army barracks on the site. The extraordinary natural beauty of the setting – 25 metres up a cliff overlooking St Bride's Bay – inspired Future Systems to design a building with an emphasis on the quality of the interior spaces and the view. From outside, the house is barely visible, shielded as it is by earth banks and a turf roof. When the planting matures, the building will blend into the landscape, just like a war-time bunker or romantic ruin. The only evidence of the structure will be the full-height glazed entrance at the rear and the elliptical glass facade, which is like a 'lens' cut into the cliff face. This site-specific response to the landscape impressed local planners who wholeheartedly approved of the project.

The house is planned with a bedroom at each end screened from the central living space by two bathroom pods. One of these also incorporates kitchen facilities. Like those in the Hauer–King house (see p46) the spray-painted timber structures were prefabricated and arrived on site with fittings and appliances installed. The opening portholes in the glazing panels are proprietary products usually used on boats.

glass and grass

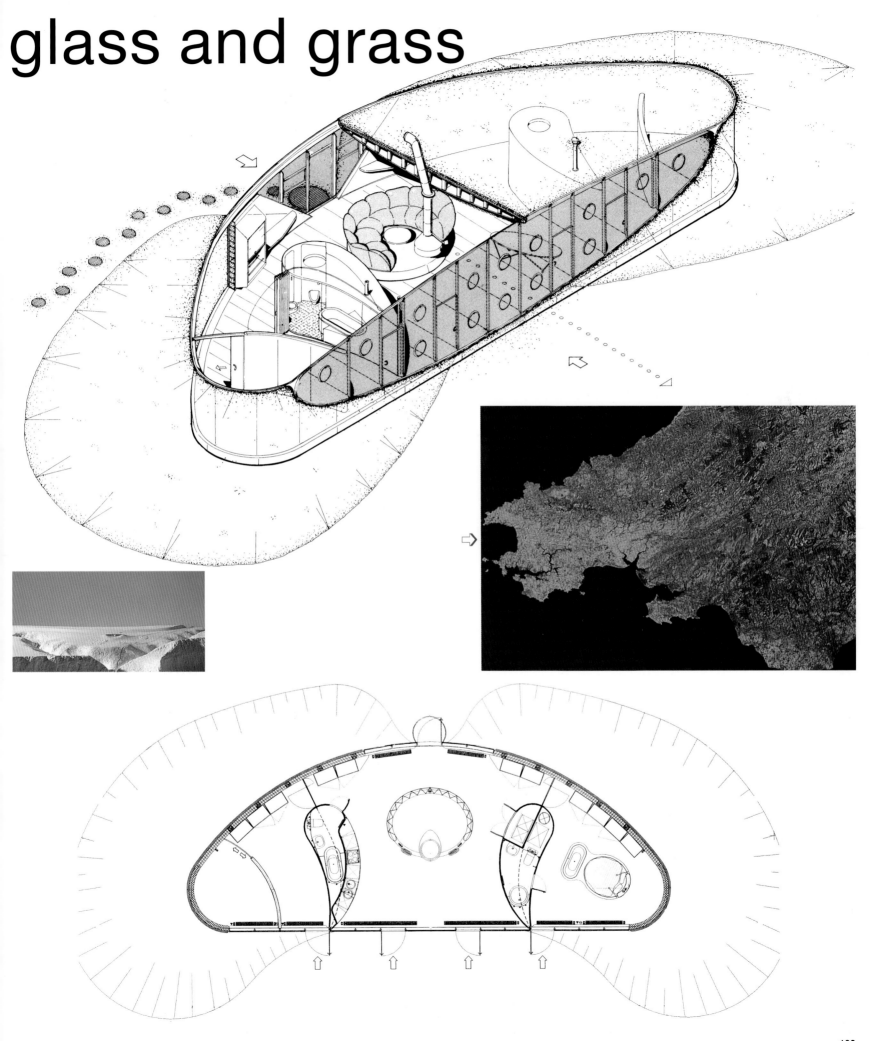

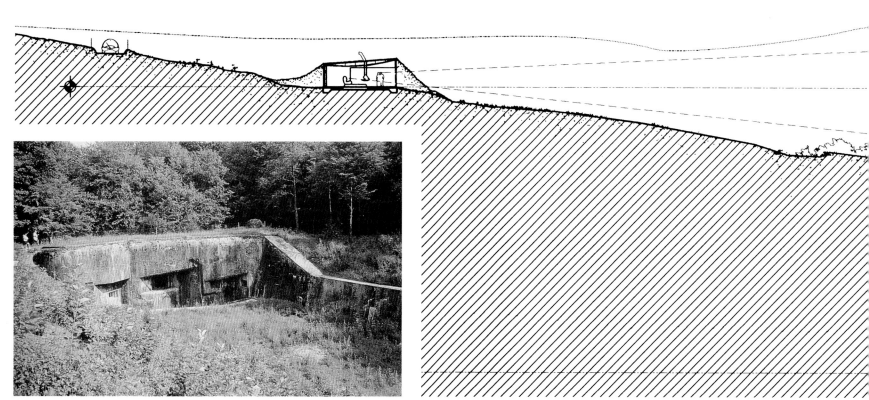

invisibility

It has long been a frustration to the architects that contemporary houses are furnished with Modern Movement furniture. Rather than use such pieces for this project, they have custom-designed a sofa, which is raised on a dais around a log fire. It seats large numbers and makes a perfect setting for entertaining.

To build the house, the site was excavated for the construction of a concrete slab and retaining wall. Onto this structure a stressed-skin ply roof was laid, complete with membrane and turf planting. The glazing panels and their steel supports complete the remainder of the structure. Underfloor heating in the slab warms the house, while double glazing and earth shielding retain the heat in winter and keep the house cool in summer.

This modest building sets many precedents for domestic architecture. It illustrates how environmentally sensitive buildings can be innovative in design, challenges conventional construction methods and realizes some of Future Systems' early ambitions. With increased levels of mass-production and prefabrication, such alternative housing might also be as competitively priced as conventional speculative units.

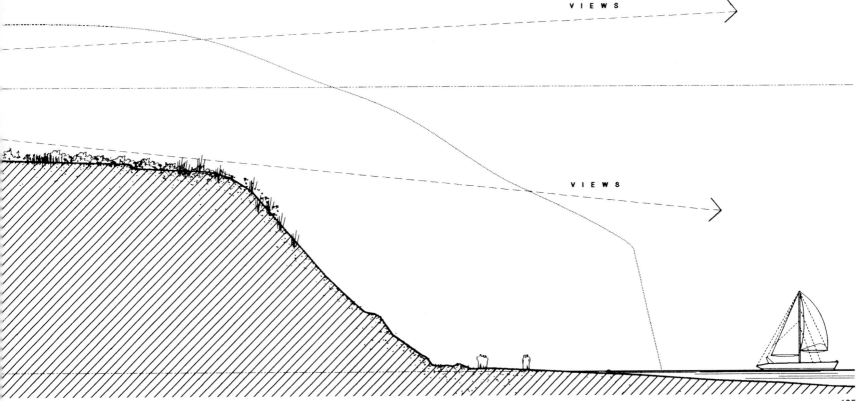

VIEWS

VIEWS

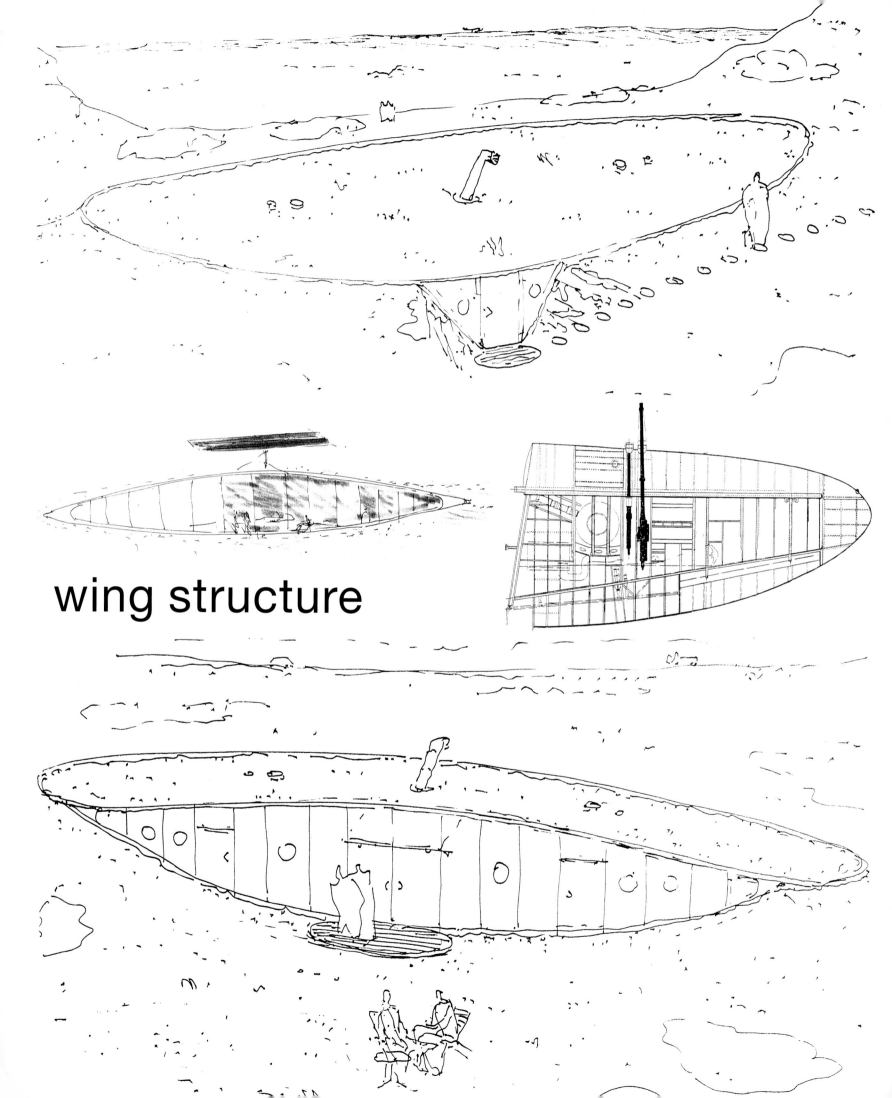

wing structure

inside

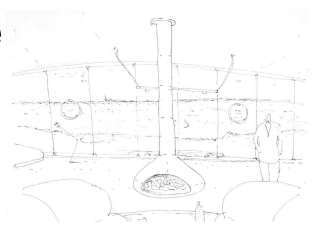

FAMILY HOUSE • CONCRETE AND BLOCKWORK
RETAINING WALL • PLYWOOD ROOF • 2 GLASS WALLS
• GRASS BANKS • 2 PREFABRICATED BATHROOMS
AND KITCHEN PODS

WIDTH	24M
DEPTH	8.4M
HEIGHT	3.1M
FLOOR AREA	150M²
STRUCTURE	TECHNIKER
ENVIRONMENTAL	BDSP
CONSTRUCTION	YOUNG CONSTRUCTION

224 THE ARK

1995

This competition-winning design will be the centrepiece of the Earth Centre, a new institution dedicated to communicating environmental issues to the public. The site for the building is an artificial landscape of former opencast mines near Doncaster, South Yorkshire. As a development of Future Systems' earlier ideas about large-scale buildings for public exhibition, including the Museum of the Acropolis and the Gallery for the 21st Century, the Ark is conceived as a series of terraced galleries stacked under a vast single-span roof. The butterfly form of this roof evolved to resemble a giant pair of colourful insect eyes nestling in the landscape.

In addition to being a striking piece of contemporary architecture, the Ark will be an environmental model. The Ark is orientated towards the south to gain warmth in cooler months, but at the same time the roof incorporates shading devices to protect it from the power of overhead mid-summer sun. The roof is conceived to provide maximum possible benefits. Photovoltaic cells are incorporated to generate free electricity and a network of 'shells' is custom-designed to filter light into the building and reduce the need for artificial sources. The double-skinned roof, which is designed as a tensile cable-net structure, also collects rainwater that can be treated and stored in underground tanks for use in flushing WCs and irrigating the surrounding landscape, which is in keeping with the principles of the Earth Centre. The roof rests on the lower part of the structure that is made of heavy concrete and bedded into the steep landscape to the north.

For much of the year the building can be naturally ventilated, with windows and doors opened to allow cool air to enter and rise up through the space and out again via the roof vents. This is supplemented by a mechanical system that draws cool air from the north side of the building through underground pipes and releases it into the deepest part of the space and high-occupancy areas such as auditoria.

roof

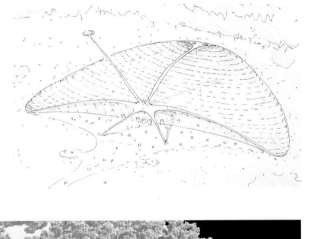

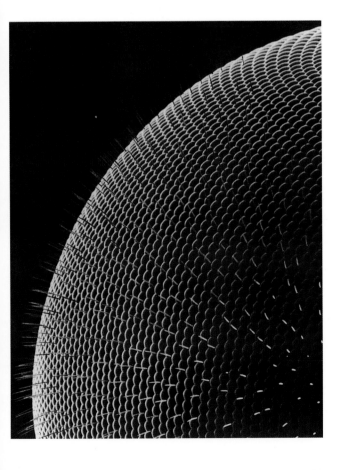

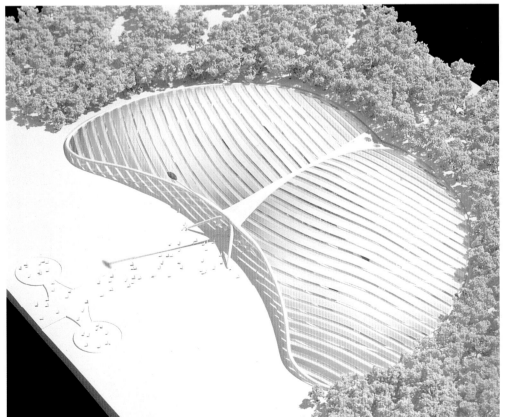

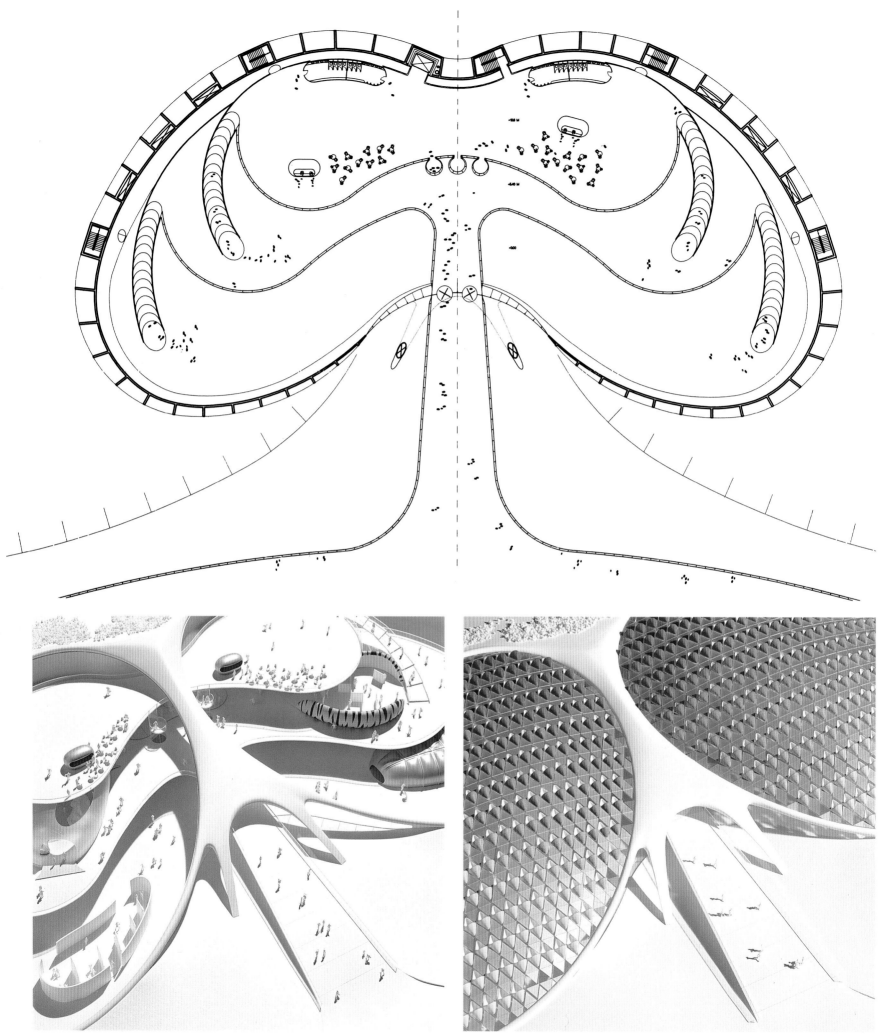

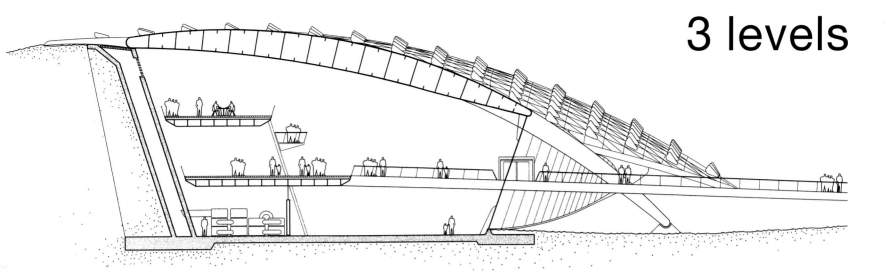

3 levels

ECOLOGICAL EXHIBITION BUILDING ON 3 LEVELS •
CONCRETE RETAINING WALL • STEEL GLAZED ROOF
• ALUMINIUM DEFLECTORS • SOLAR CELLS •
RETRACTABLE FRONT GLASS WALL

LENGTH	125M
WIDTH	62M
HEIGHT	18M
FLOOR AREA	10,000M²
STRUCTURE	OVE ARUP & PARTNERS
ENVIRONMENT	OVE ARUP & PARTNERS
STATUS	COMPLETION 2002

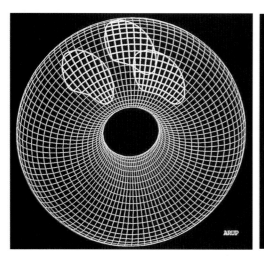
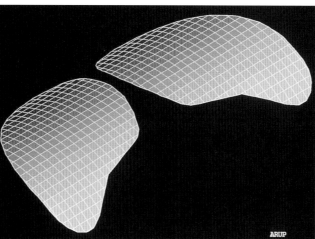
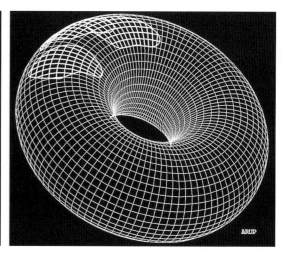

form-finding

In the winter the building is warmed by rays of sun passing over the glass roof, a source of heat which is also recovered from the highest part of the space via extract chimneys and used to heat incoming fresh air. Perimeter radiators powered by gas boilers provide supplementary heating. Warm water for use in catering and WCs will be heated by solar power.

Apart from its ambitious agenda for energy efficiency, the building is intended to be an inspiring example of the best in modern architecture. From the outside the building will form a dramatic and unconventional image, especially at night when it will emit a seductive glow. The drama is continued inside as the visitor experiences the grand non-orthogonal spaces and exciting interactive exhibits (even the sweeping staircases linking the terraced galleries are reminiscent of those in old Hollywood films).

For Future Systems the building of the Ark (which at the time of writing has been awarded funding by the Millennium Commission and is awaiting matching funds from the private sector) would mark a significant stage in the development of their work. With its glazed roof and heavy base it displays very different technology from the Media Centre at Lord's and shows the diversity of the team's approach. But according to Amanda Levete, its most important achievement is as an example of good 'green' architecture in a financially deprived part of Britain, which has both a social function and is genuinely public.

seasons

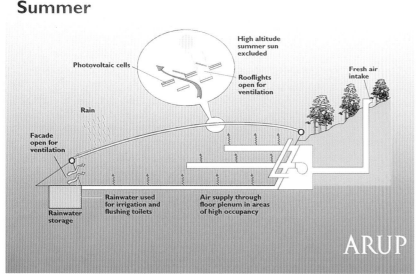

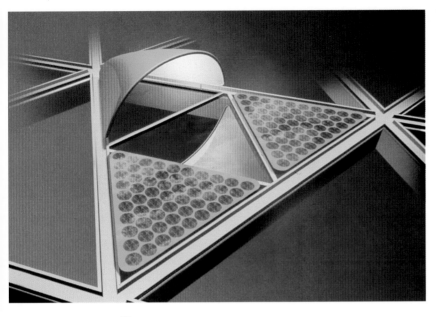

roof systems

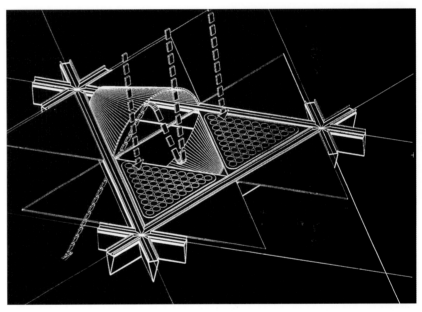

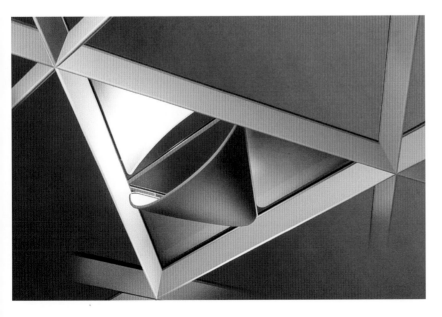

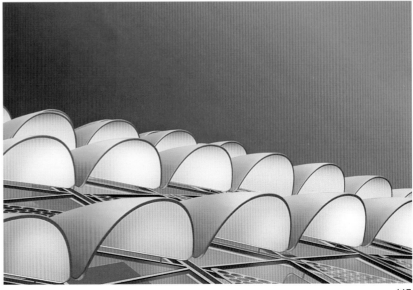

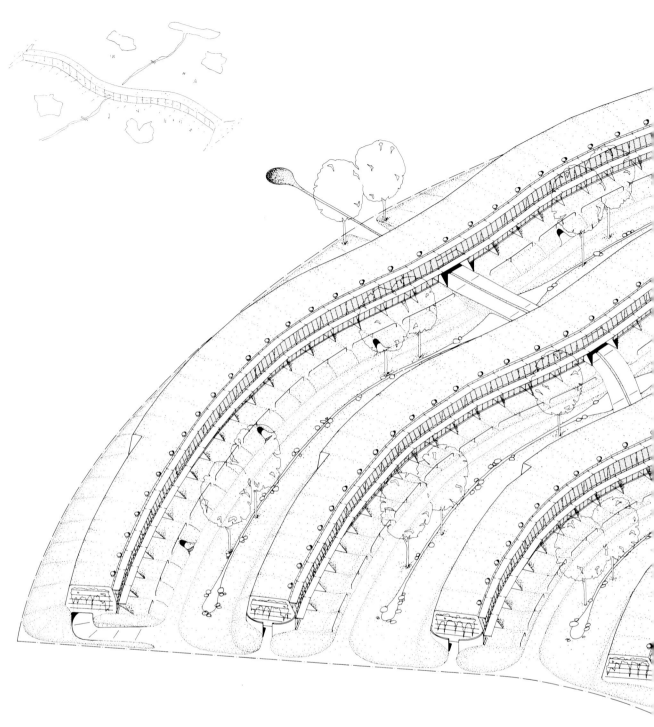

225 LINZ HOUSING

1995

with the Richard Rogers Partnership

One of Future Systems' primary interests is in housing, particularly in exploring the potential for affordable, high-quality, 'green' accommodation for ordinary people. (Their built and unbuilt schemes for individual houses all contain ideas which would be applicable to larger-scale housing projects.) Given that funding for research in this area is scarce, the architects were pleased to be invited to develop ideas for such a scheme by the Austrian city of Linz, partly funded by the European Commission.

The site is in a wooded setting close to a tram stop just outside the city. Future Systems collaborated with architects from the Richard Rogers Partnership to develop a scheme for terraced houses where the emphasis

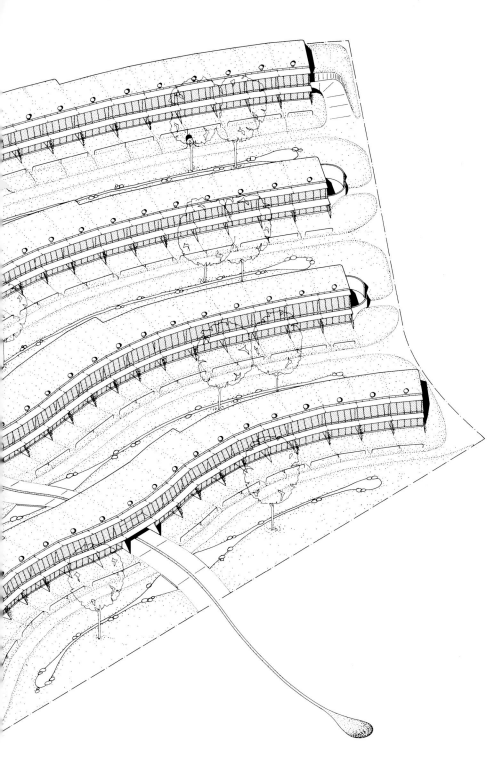

ecological buildings

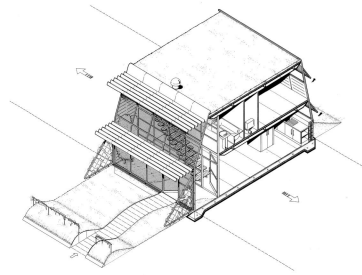

159 units

is on quality of experience and space, as well as a concern for the environment. Each concrete-framed house is designed with a double-height atrium on the south-facing facade. This generates warmth in winter and provides an airy buffer zone in summer. Roofs of the curving terraces are planted with grass and emphasis is placed on landscaping the sites between the buildings.

A number of different-sized units provides variety in the layout of houses and flexibility for the size of the families who will occupy them. Given that many people use cars to travel to and from the city, parking is provided in underground carparks at the rear of the site.

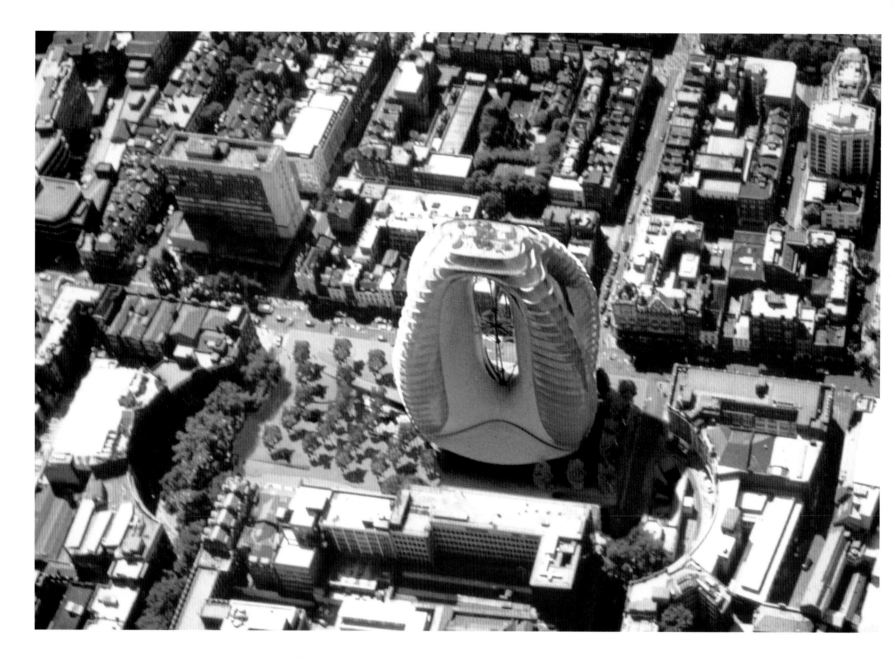

226 PROJECT ZED, LONDON

1995

Project Zed, London is one of three speculative mixed-used developments designed by Future Systems in collaboration with the Martin Centre at Cambridge University and a team of engineering consultants. The three projects were all developed with funding from the European Commission. The ambition here is to make a building containing offices, apartments and shops which is both energy-efficient and architecturally inspiring.
On a site just off Tottenham Court Road, the team proposed an elegant 26-storey building with retail spaces on the lower floors, offices above and three floors of apartments and a swimming pool at the top. 'The building is set in a park, so we went high to give as much public space at the bottom as possible,' explains Kaplicky.
Cut through the centre of the steel-framed building is a giant turbine which generates free electricity by harnessing the power of the wind. Photovoltaic cells located in the louvers generate power from the sun. The idea is that the building should be almost entirely self-sufficient in terms of energy. The curved facade, composed of triangulated glass panels, is designed to reduce the impact of the wind at the edges and to drive it through the turbine at the centre.

generator

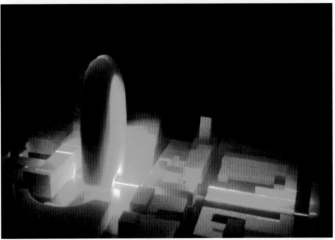

ENERGY-EFFICIENT HIGH-RISE OFFICE AND RESIDENTIAL
BUILDING • SHOPS • STEEL STRUCTURE • MINIMAL FOOTPRINT
• 2 VERTICAL GENERATORS • LARGE PARK • CAR PARK

HEIGHT	107M
LENGTH	67M
NUMBER OF FLOORS	25
FLOOR AREA	27,600M²
STRUCTURE	TECHNIKER
ENVIRONMENTAL	BDSP
STATUS	EU RESEARCH PROJECT

APAS London Scheme II Daylight Factor Contours 13th floor

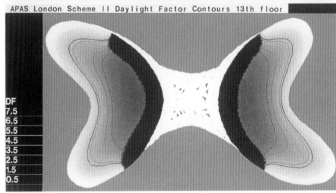

DF
7.5
6.5
5.5
4.5
3.5
2.5
1.5
0.5

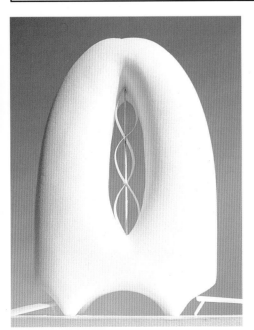

windmill

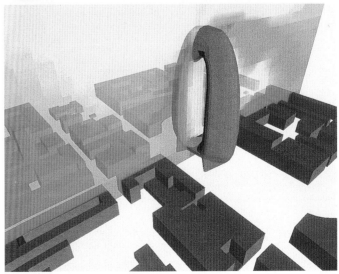

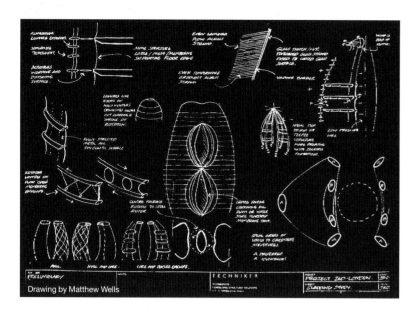

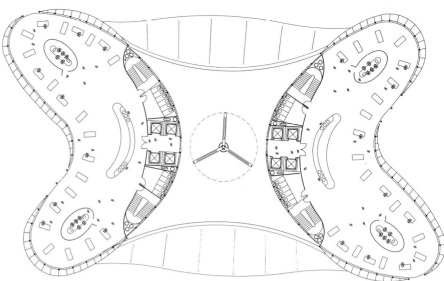

Inside the building the butterfly-shaped plan allows for unusual and exhilarating office spaces which are naturally ventilated and daylit on each side. Services such as lifts and WCs are located along the walls facing the turbine. The apartments at the top of the building vary in size, to take advantage of views out with living areas placed along the glazed facades and bathrooms contained in prefabricated pods at the rear.

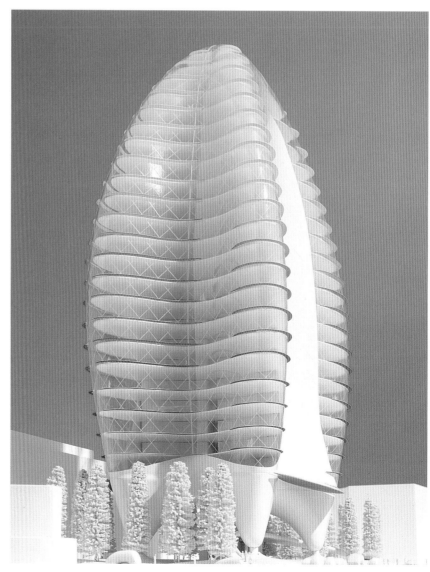

228 PROJECT ZED, TOULOUSE

1995

Like Project Zed, London and Project Zed, Berlin this collaborative scheme is designed to illustrate the potential for energy-efficient mixed-use developments containing offices and apartments. Project Zed, Toulouse is a response to the temperate climate of the French city. The building is designed around an atrium, making the floors shallow in plan and providing pleasant views on all aspects.

To make best use of the sunny weather, solar panels and photovoltaic cells have been incorporated into the skin of the building to generate free power. The surface area of the exterior has also been maximized by rippling the plan and elevations. This allows the heat to be more efficiently dissipated and is also a self-shading device. In addition it makes the volumes of the spaces inside more interesting (a particular benefit for the apartments on the upper level in which the ceilings are also curved).

A heavy structure is proposed for this project, including innovative ceramic cladding. The theory is that this would cool down at night and absorb heat during the day, limiting requirements for mechanical cooling. Natural ventilation is provided via opening windows at low and high levels.

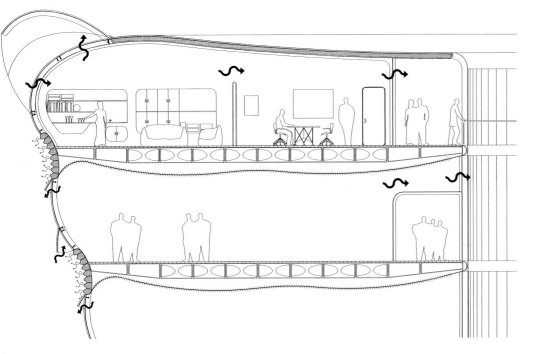

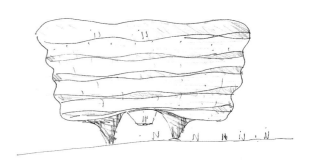

ENERGY-EFFICIENT OFFICE AND RESIDENTIAL
BUILDING • 5 STOREYS • CENTRAL CORE • STEEL
STRUCTURE • CERAMIC CLADDING

HEIGHT	27M
WIDTH	46M
FLOOR AREA	5,700M²
STRUCTURE	TECHNIKER
ENVIRONMENTAL	BDSP
CONSTRUCTION	EU RESEARCH PROJECT

229 PROJECT ZED, BERLIN 1995

This third scheme is the final Project Zed collaboration to explore new ideas for ecological mixed-use developments in European cities.

Half of the city-centre site for this project has been planned as public parkland. Two curving lines of low-rise (21 metres high), shallow-plan buildings (11 metres deep) are partially dug into the earth to insulate them in winter and cool them in summer. Meanwhile, maximum benefit is gained from glazed facades, incorporating solar panels and photovoltaic panels, oriented towards the sun. Opening windows provide natural ventilation, with warm air passing out through a duct at the rear of the building. Rainwater collected from the roofs is stored in tanks in the earth banks and used for flushing sanitary fittings. Carparking (ideally for 'environmentally friendly electric vehicles,' suggests Kaplicky) is provided at basement level.

Inside the buildings, the spaces are designed to challenge conventional architectural volumes (this is especially important in Berlin, where most new buildings are modelled on traditional nineteenth-century blocks). The result is achieved by the use of curving plans, roofs and elevations that add interest to the spaces of everyday life.

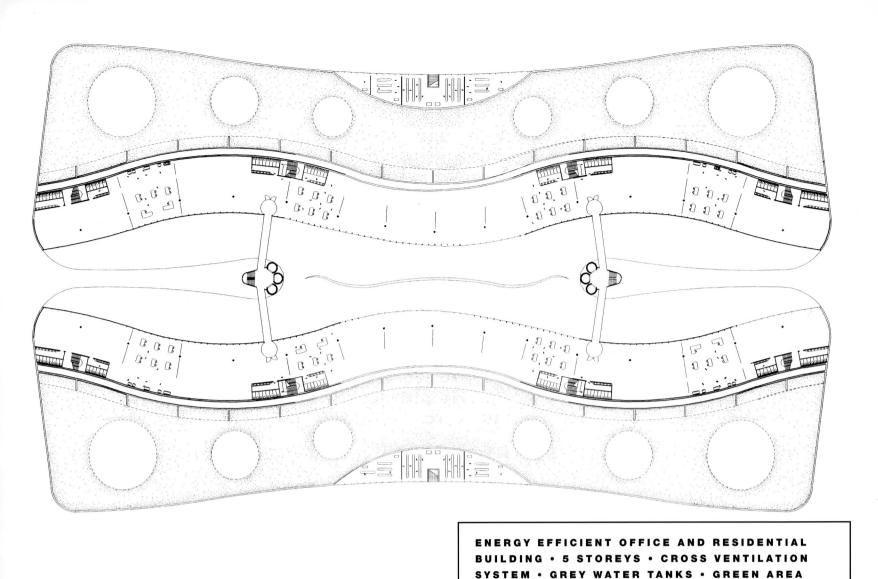

ENERGY EFFICIENT OFFICE AND RESIDENTIAL
BUILDING • 5 STOREYS • CROSS VENTILATION
SYSTEM • GREY WATER TANKS • GREEN AREA
• CAR PARK

HEIGHT	**18M**
LENGTH	**216M**
FLOOR AREA	**22,000M²**
STRUCTURE	**TECHNIKER**
ENVIRONMENTAL	**BDSP**
STATUS	**EU RESEARCH PROJECT**

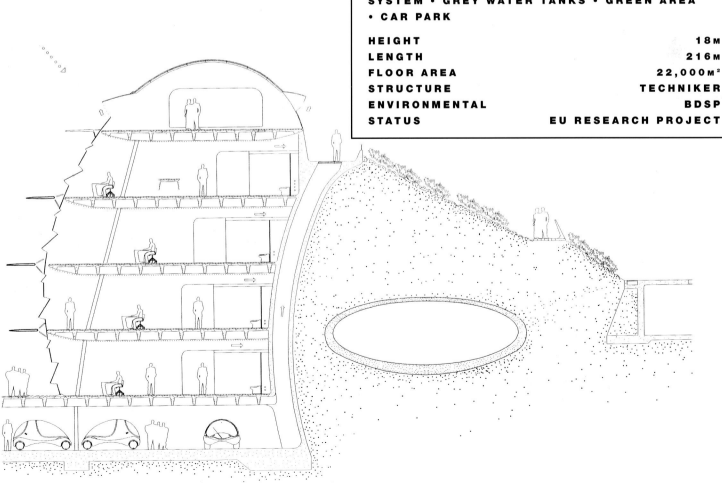

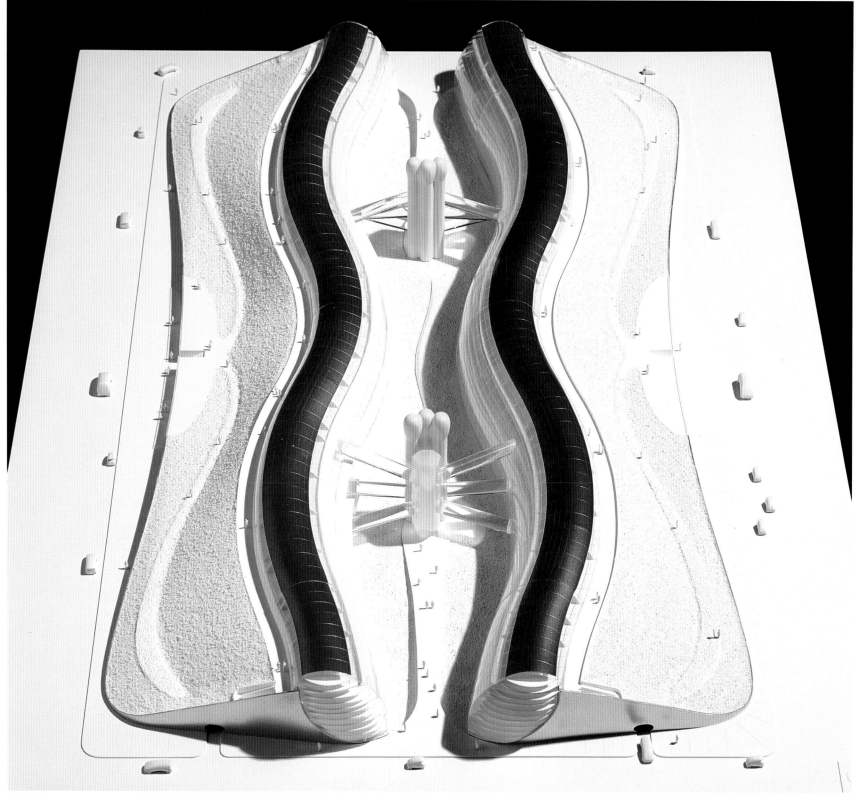

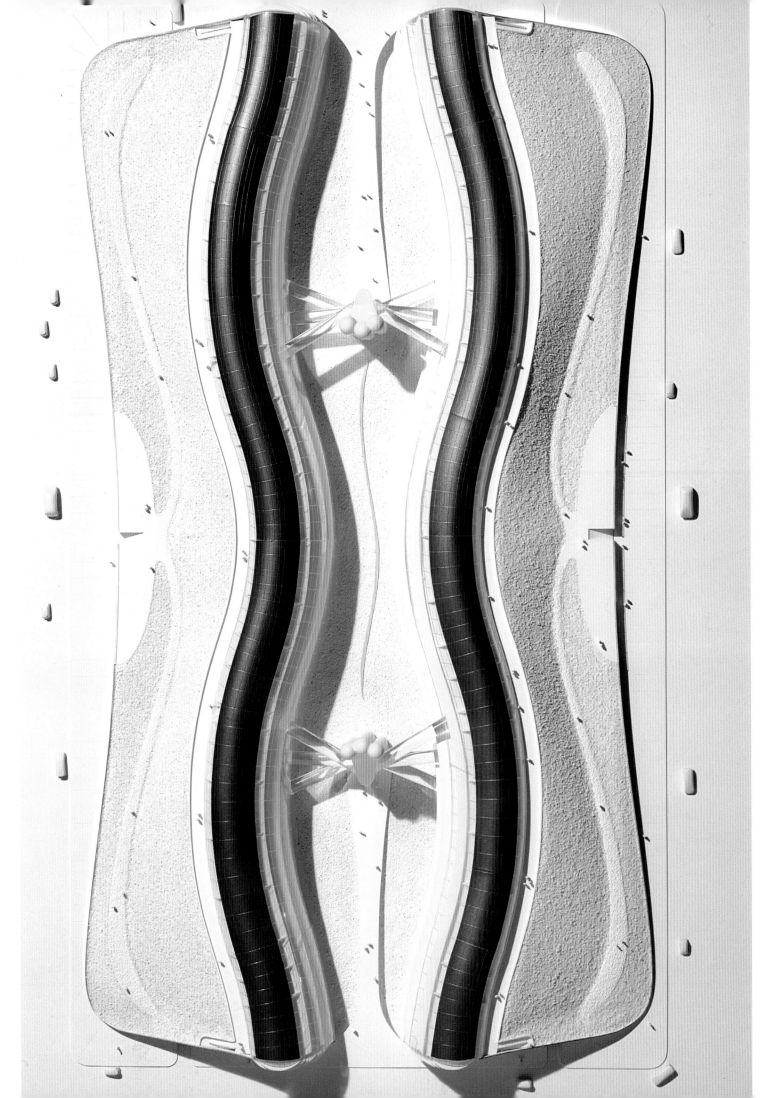

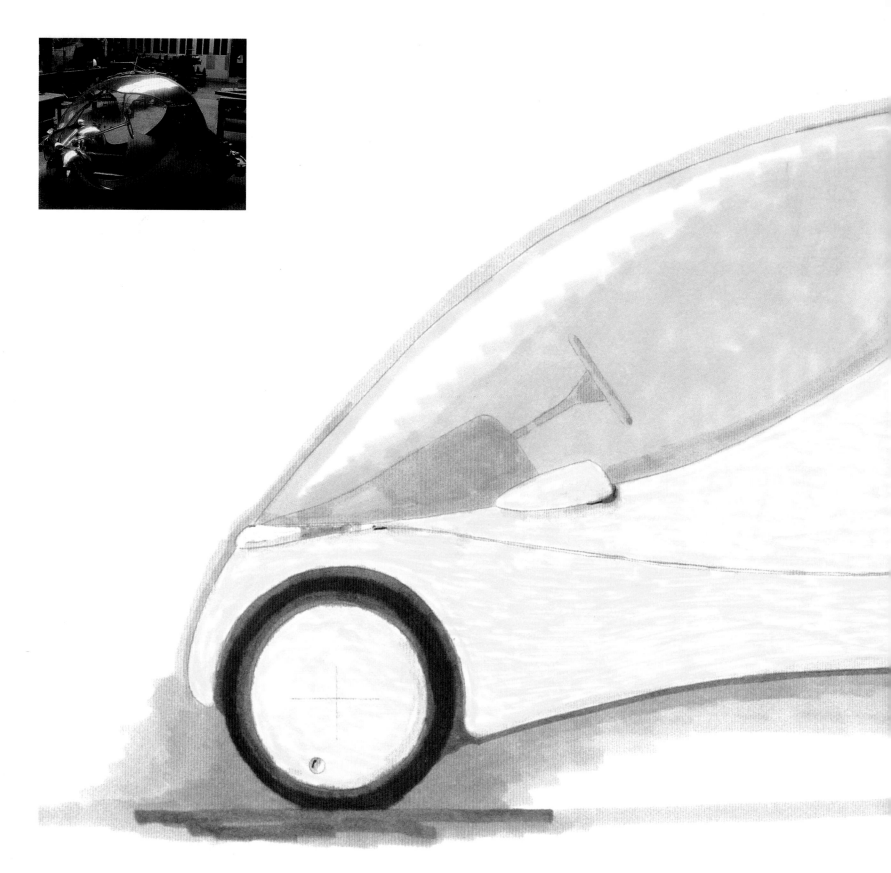

232 ELECTRIC CAR 1995

3-metre long electric car • 3 adults, 1 child • central driver's position • lightweight monocoque plastic body • panoramic views • four electric motors and advanced batteries • maximum weight 300 kg • luggage space

237 HILLGATE STREET   1996

For the uninitiated, finding the home of Kaplicky and Levete can be quite a challenge. This is because the house, which is in London's Notting Hill, is hidden behind an industrial looking roller-shutter sandwiched between two smart townhouses. But then Kaplicky and Levete, the entrance reminds us, are not conventional people ('I could never live behind a front door like that,' says Kaplicky of the flanking thresholds).

Beyond the roller-shutter and small covered yard is a large, light-filled house that has been modelled out of a very ordinary 1950s light industrial building. With a minimal budget and fast-track programme, Future Systems stripped out the rabbit warren of offices which previously occupied the space and re-planned the building to create a series of living zones. Existing services partly dictated the location of bathroom and kitchen at the front of the ground floor, with dining and sleeping zones to the rear. A new aluminium-plate staircase leads to a large living room and study area on the first floor.

Both Kaplicky and Levete have long supported the idea of free and open-plan living, a concept which is clear in their work and in their home. There are only three doors in this house; the front door, a door for the WC and another for their son's bedroom. The bathroom, kitchen and main bedroom are zoned by partitions which stop well below ceiling height while the rest of the house is entirely open.

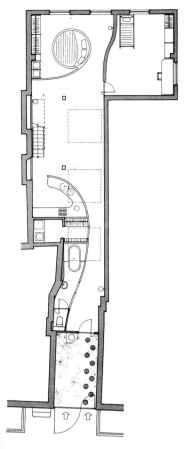

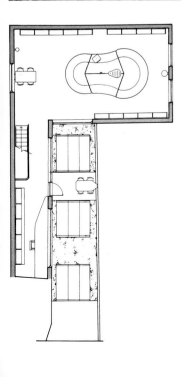

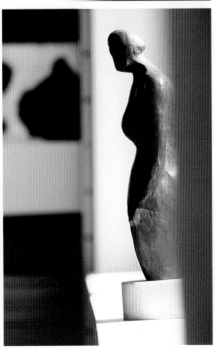

200m² ersatz architecture

The interior, which is largely top-lit at ground floor level, is an exhilarating space. This feeling is heightened by the lemon-yellow partitions and the custom-dyed 'hot-lips' pink carpet. For Kaplicky and Levete the house functions as a kind of testing ground for ideas. The circular aluminium dining table and beds on the ground floor and the large and inviting seating 'dinghy' on the first floor are all Future Systems projects.

'This project was interesting for both of us,' says Levete. 'Because of the limited budget it wasn't about the quality of finishes or the details, but about having a simple idea and making it work spatially. We had to turn a blind eye to an enormous amount, but I found that quite liberating in a way.' Thus the water from the roof still drains through internal pipes and the existing windows are not what the architects would choose, but the overall concept has been realized. 'I think it's quite successful as a living space,' she concludes. 'It allows you to be quite messy and to use the space freely without it dictating. How you apply that to larger buildings I think is interesting.'

after

240 HABITABLE BRIDGE 1996

In 1996 a number of leading architects were invited by the Royal Academy of Arts in London to submit designs for a habitable bridge to cross the River Thames. The brief was for a structure containing retail and other public spaces. Submitted designs were exhibited as models at the Academy's popular exhibition 'Living Bridges'. Future Systems' scheme for a 'people's bridge' is inspired by historic precedents, including the famous Ponte Vecchio in Florence and the Charles Bridge in Prague which is filled with strolling crowds in summer. Natural forces and structures like the tidal movement of the river and a slender bridge of rock in Utah, USA, also provided inspiration for the elegant form.

Because of the unpredictable nature of the British climate, the bridge is conceived mainly as an enclosed structure. Several decks, like those of a ship, are stacked inside, with the top route open to the sky. Restaurants and bars line the decks and panoramic views are provided up and down the river and to the historic landmarks on the banks. The 475-metre long bridge (longer than the Eiffel Tower turned on its side or the *Queen Mary*) would be built as a semi-monocoque structure, an appropriate form given its close affinity with the ships and boats on the river. Like the footbridge at West India Quay, its steel sections would be pre-fabricated to ensure efficiency of manufacture and quality of finish.

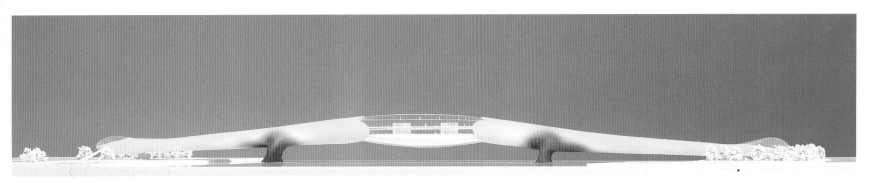

3-SPAN PEDESTRIAN BRIDGE • 2-LEVEL CROSSING
SHOPS AND RESTAURANTS • VIEWING PLATFORMS
SEMI-MONOCOQUE STEEL STRUCTURE • SHIPYARD
PREFABRICATION

SPAN	450M
WIDTH	36M
STRUCTURE	TECHNIKER
STATUS	INVITED COMPETITION

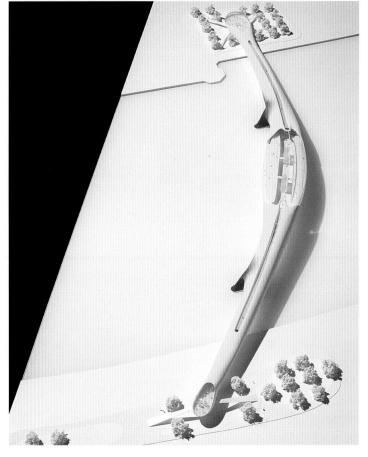

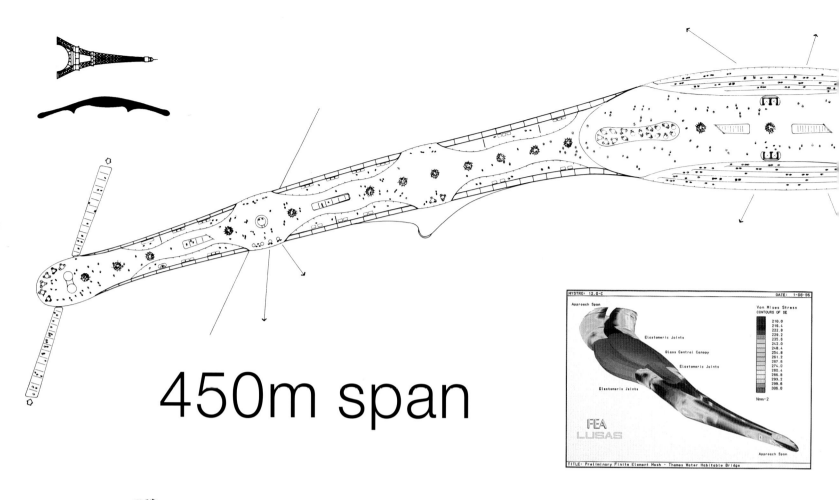

450m span

shops

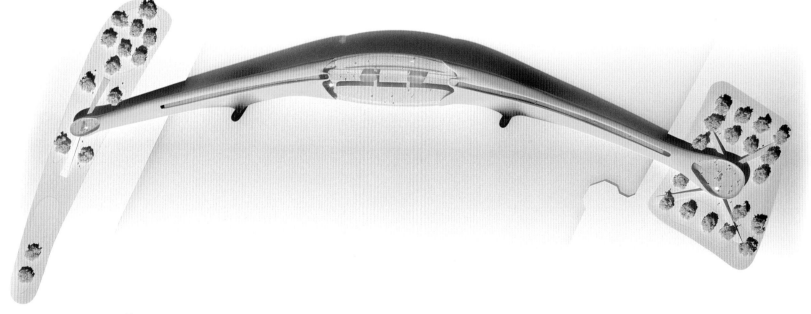

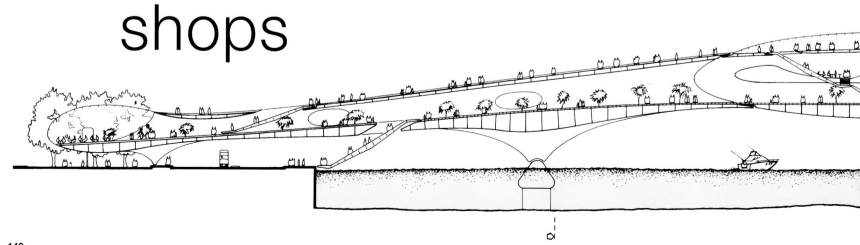

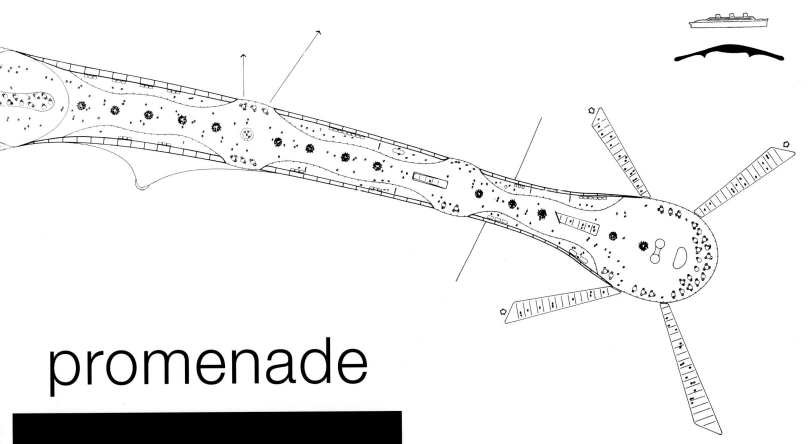

promenade

restaurant garden

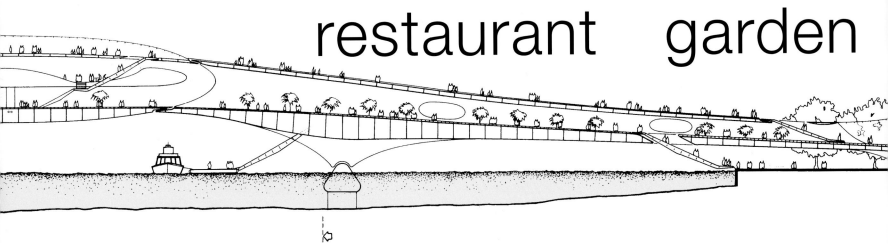

242 HALLFIELD SCHOOL 1996

In 1996 Future Systems was invited to take part in a competition to extend Hallfield Primary School, a landmark building in Paddington, London, designed by Denys Lasdun. 'It was interesting, because the competition was not just about Hallfield, but about designing a system of classrooms which could also be used in other locations,' explains Levete. The practice's winning scheme proposes a series of six circular buildings, each divided into two classrooms, linked by a snaking corridor. 'It is a poetic response to the site,' says Levete. The units are prefabricated, with the potential for mass production. In the initial proposal the roof and slab were pre-cast concrete, but other materials such as aluminium or timber are also being explored. A spine wall cuts through each building, acting as a partition, service duct and storage facility. The classrooms are naturally ventilated through floors and roofs. Careful consideration has been paid to energy efficiency. Partly, the ambition for this project is to provide maximum daylight and good views for the users. Full daylight is achieved by making the classrooms top-lit, filtered by a suspended fabric screen, which allows an even quality of light to penetrate deep into the plan. The emphasis for the windows is to frame the views out. Designed for nursery-age children, the windows are low-level and the ceiling height is a modest 2.4 metres. In response to lingering doubts about prefabricated mass-produced buildings, Future Systems claims that the advantages of high-quality production and reduced costs outweigh any negative aspects. Although the scheme remains unbuilt, the urgent need for high-quality nursery environments in Britain means that Future Systems is keen to develop this idea further and research on the project continues.

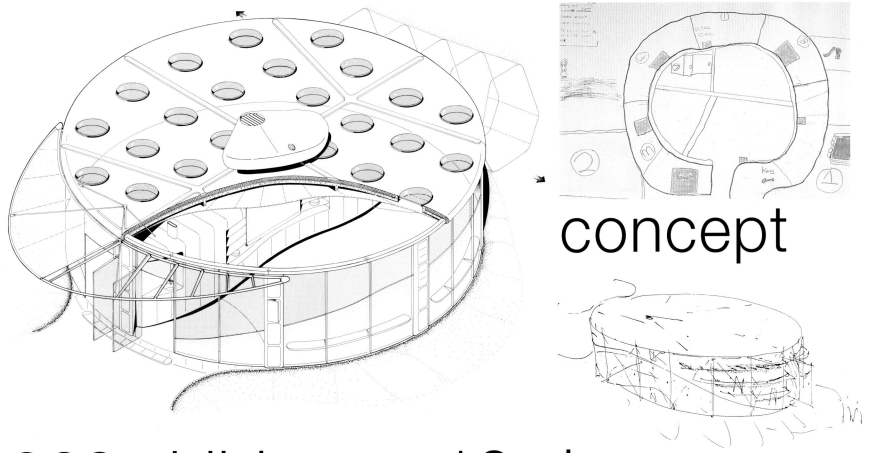

concept

360 children   12 classrooms

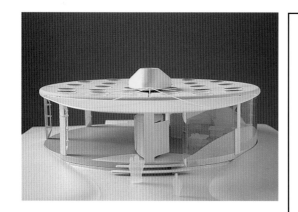

PREFABRICATED 2-CLASSROOM UNIT •
LIGHTWEIGHT ALUMINIUM STRUCTURE •
INSULATED GLASS WALL • TOP LIGHT •
NATURAL VENTILATION • STORAGE SYSTEM

DIAMETER	12m
HEIGHT	2.7m
FLOOR AREA	113m²
STRUCTURE	OVE ARUP & PARTNERS
ENVIRONMENT	OVE ARUP & PARTNERS
STATUS	COMPETITION WIN

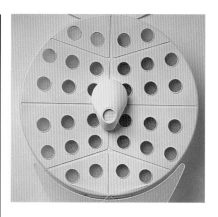

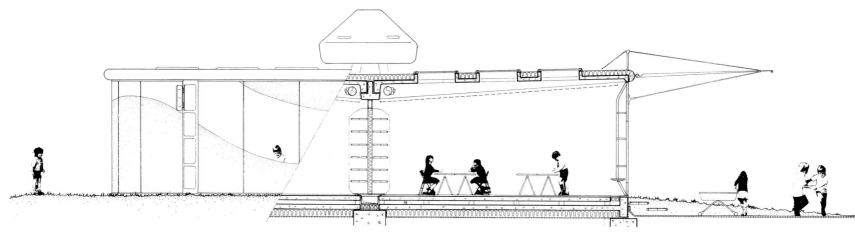

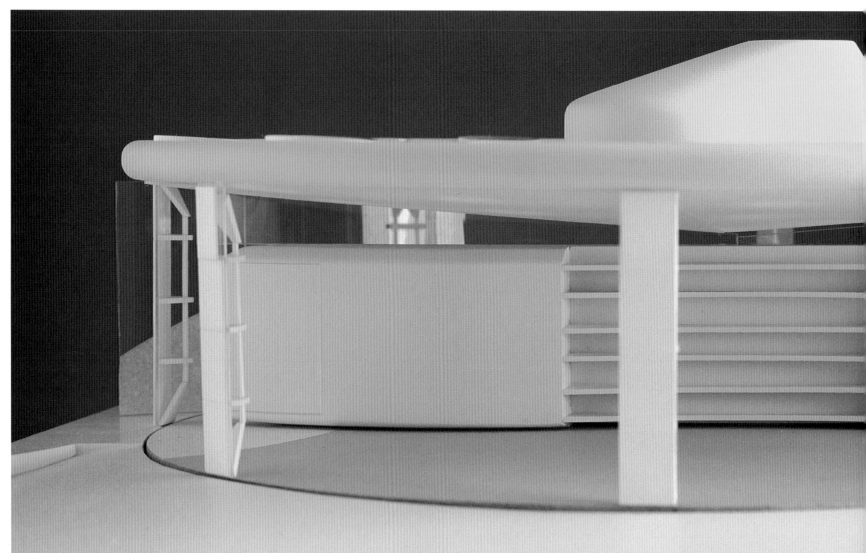

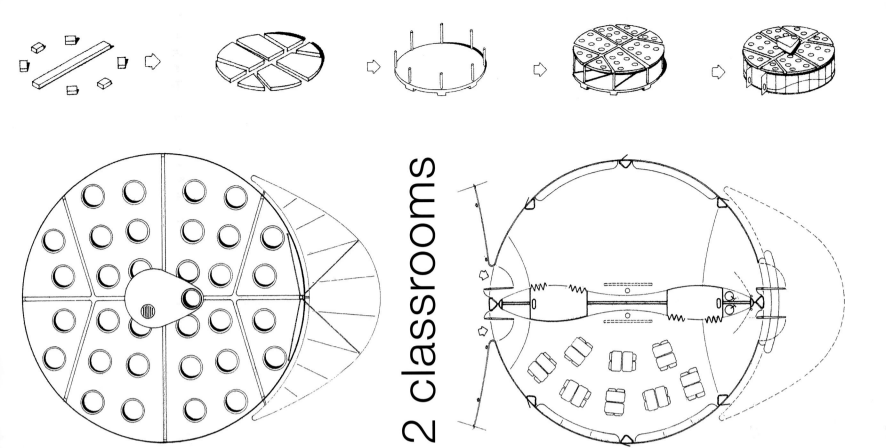

2 classrooms

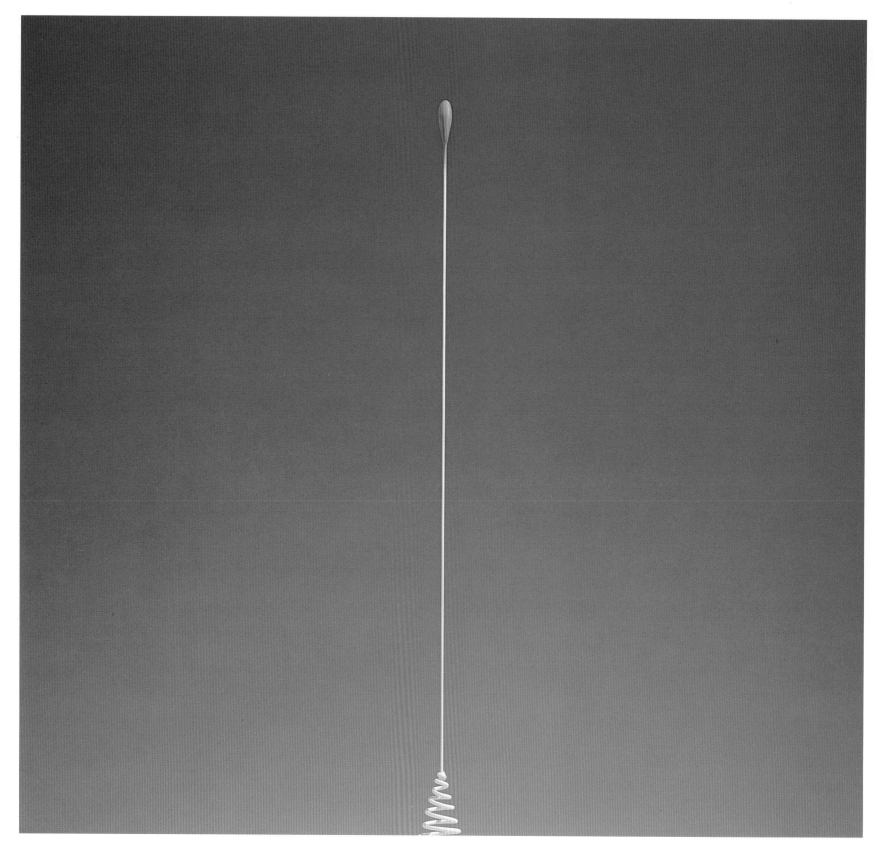

246 1997

CONSTRUCTION TOWER

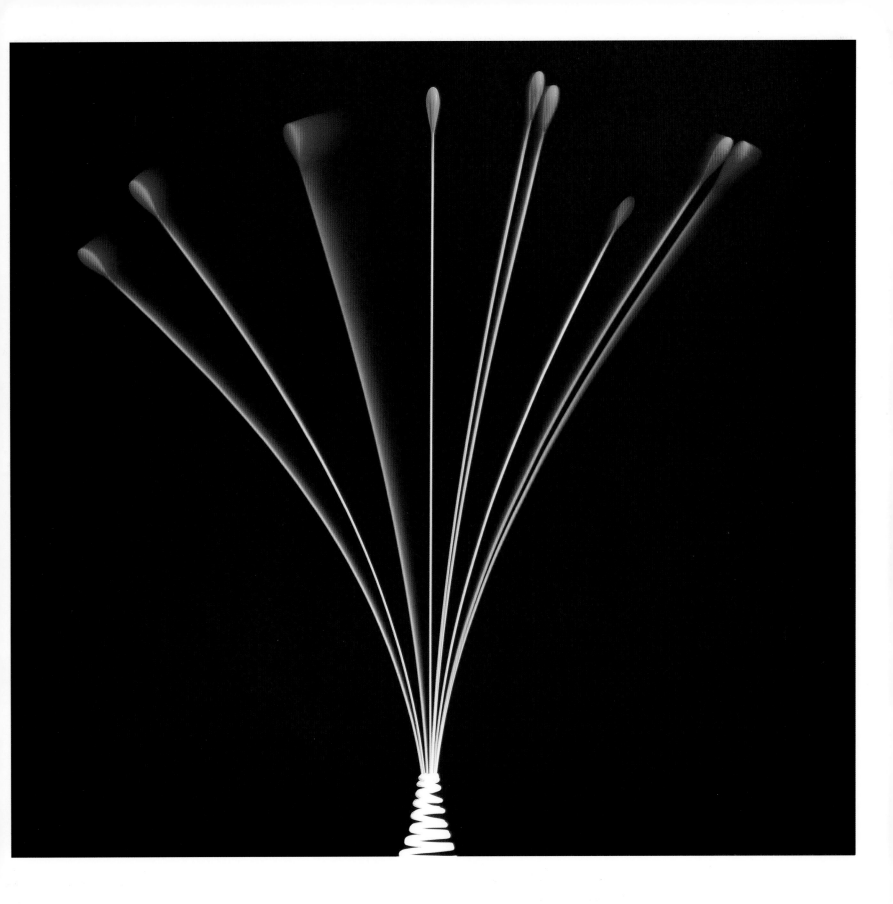

competition project • dynamic structure • a pendulum free to oscillate • lighted tip highlights movement

249 FLOWER SHOP 1997

The striking facade of this shop in Notting Hill stands in contrast to the prevailing trend in fashionable London stores for big glass fronts framed in concrete or stainless steel. Instead it draws on the classic shops of the Modern Movement for inspiration, like those experienced by Kaplicky in the Prague of his youth or the iconic shops designed in the 1920s and 30s by Wells Coates in England.

Nicky Tibbles, the owner of Wild at Heart, already had a high-profile shop in the area (the famous blue-tiled kiosk designed by Piers Gough). For this larger shop she wanted something more formal. The idea, says Future Systems' associate Angus Pond, was to create a couture environment for flowers.

The result is a simple white interior against which the flowers stand out. Rather than showing stems in buckets, however, the display system here is conceived as a series of curving and cascading terraces. Water containers are concealed in these spray-painted mdf structures leaving nothing to distract from the blooms. In order to introduce light to the preparation area in the basement (complete with custom-designed work bench), the floor at the front of the shop has been cut back. Two curving balustrades around the new void give a glamorous sweep to the entrance. Apart from the flower containers, two other elements are built into the display system: a small seat upholstered in bright yellow vinyl and a cash desk. A projector suspended from the ceiling is intended to show a changing series of flower-related images on the rear wall.

Among the most striking features of this project is the glazed panel which sits in front of the original facade. 'We wanted to do something new and put the glass outside the frame,' explains Pond. Conceived as a 'shield', this element makes a clear distinction between what is new and what is old. The glass is spray-painted on the rear, leaving a transparent, organically shaped window in the centre.

The final element which gives this shop its distinct look is the aluminium entrance ramp. This spans over the new slot to the basement and stands in dramatic contrast to the conventional steps of neighbouring stores. It also recalls earlier Future Systems projects, such as the 1983 flat for Deyan Sudjic, and anticipates the dramatic entrance tunnel of the Comme des Garçons store in New York.

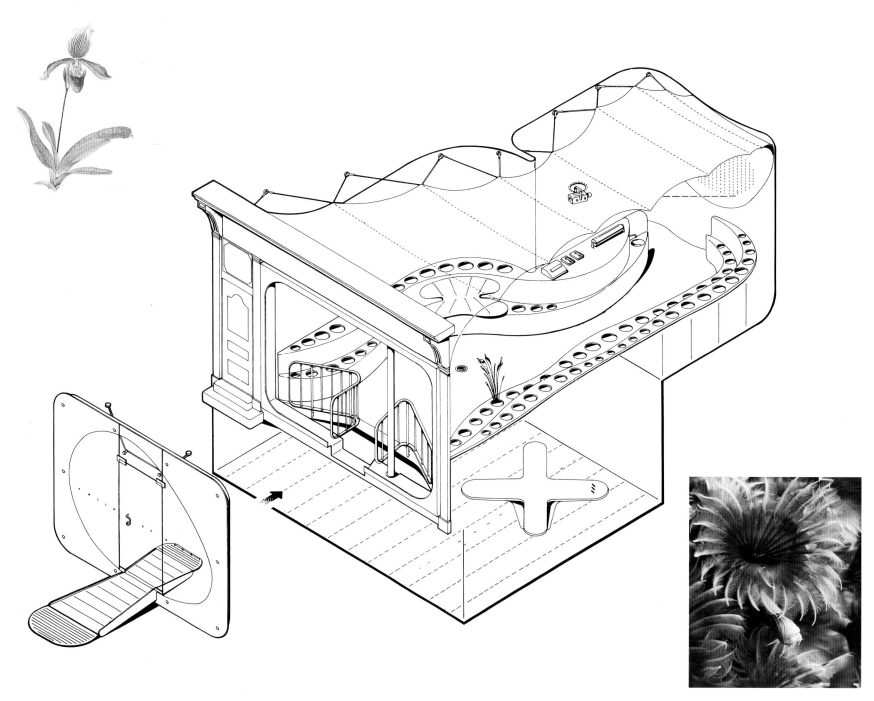

shield

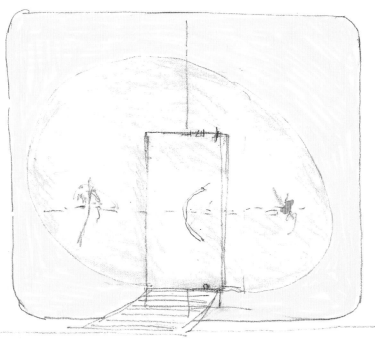

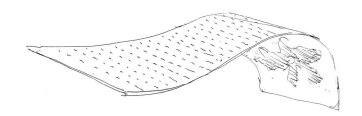

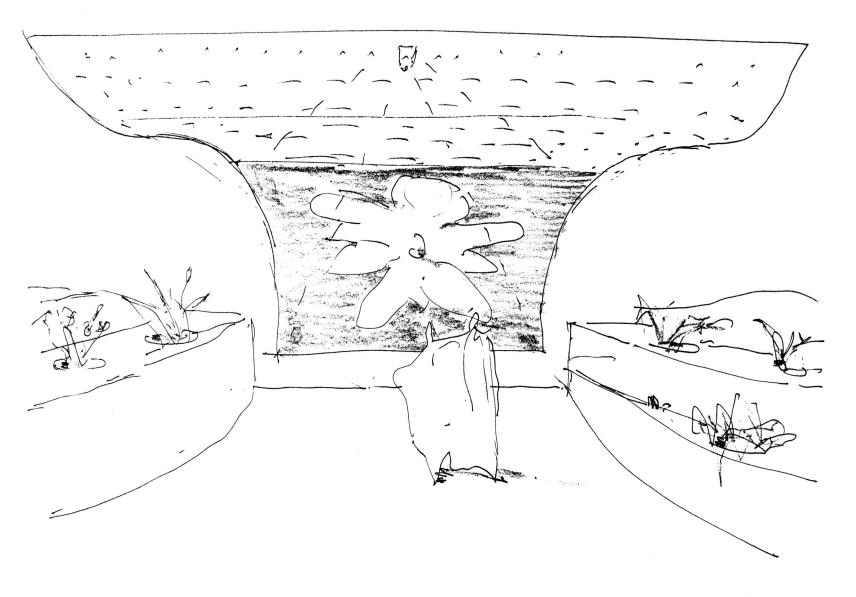

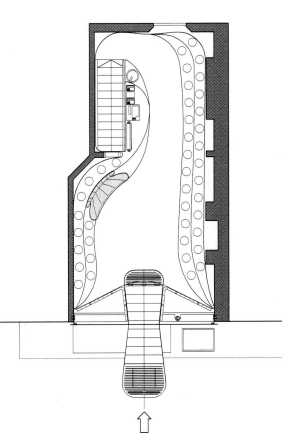

white

SHOP • PAINTED GLASS SHOPFRONT SHIELD • MDF
STEPPED INTERIOR CONSTRUCTION

WIDTH	4.2M
LENGTH	8M
FLOOR AREA	60M²
STRUCTURE	OVE ARUP & PARTNERS
CONSTRUCTION	CGN CONTRACTS

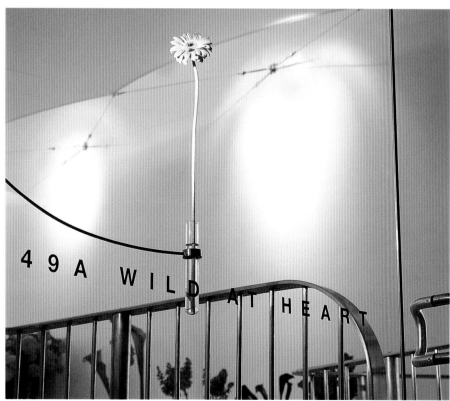

49A WILD AT HEART

yellow

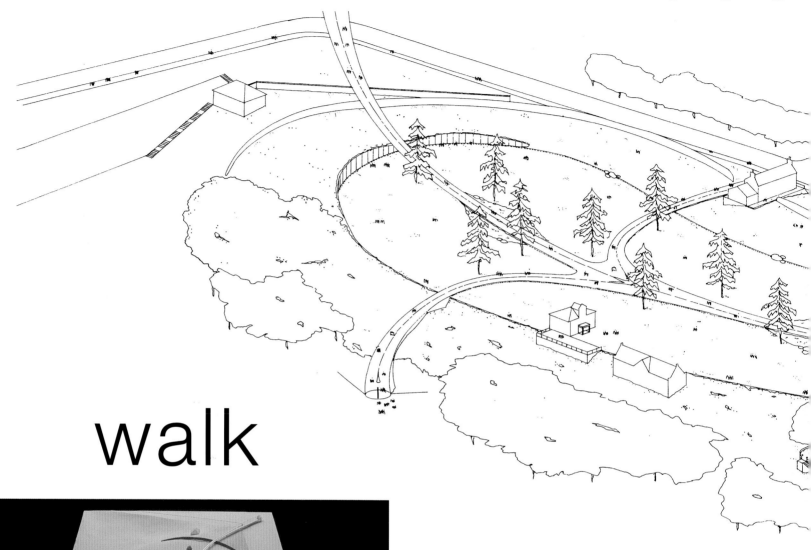

walk

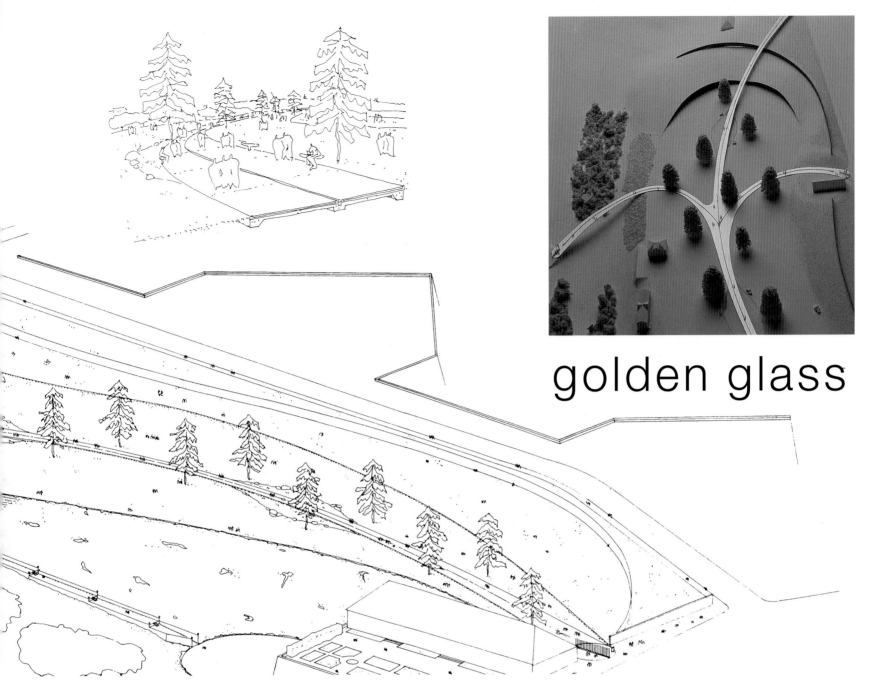

golden glass

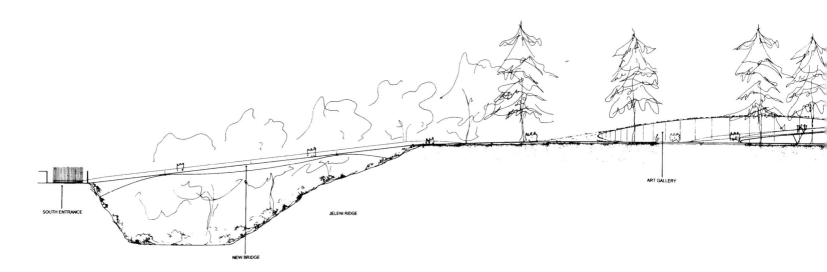

SOUTH ENTRANCE

NEW BRIDGE

JELENI RIDGE

ART GALLERY

public garden

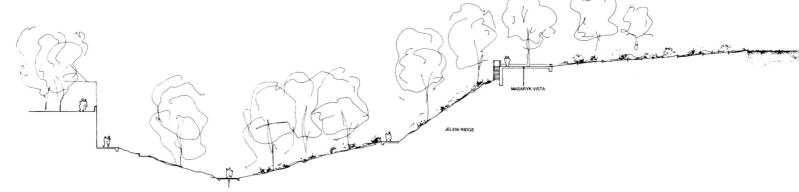

MASARYK VISTA

JELENI RIDGE

The celebrated remodelling of Prague Castle – home of the Czech government – and its surrounding gardens by the architect Joze Plecnik, undertaken in the years 1920 to 1934, has had an important influence on Jan Kaplicky and his work. He remembers visiting the castle as a child and marvelling at the bold, modern interventions, both to the interiors and to the grounds.

This scheme for the landscaping of the Pheasantry, part of the castle gardens untouched by Plecnik, is a response to a competition brief set in 1995. Here Future Systems proposed the clearing away of some inferior buildings to make way for a new park and 'golden route'.

The organic form of the park is emphasized by a series of gentle terraces that rise at one end and create curving expanses of while marble pebbles interspersed with large areas of grass. A dramatic route through this landscape – with the possibility to approach from four different directions – is created in the form of a pathway of golden glass. This colour is chosen for its rich contrast with the greenery and pebbles and as a

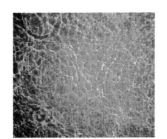

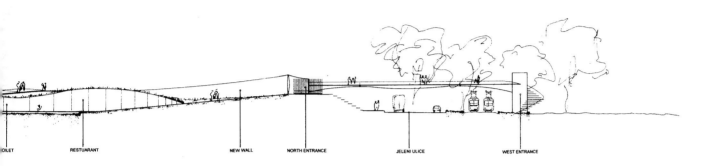

TOILET   RESTUARANT   NEW WALL   NORTH ENTRANCE   JELENI ULICE   WEST ENTRANCE

no buildings

FROM EAST ENTRANCE   NEW WALL

reference to Plecnik's work and the history of the castle (Golden Lane runs close by, the street where alchemists are rumoured to have lived). Structurally the path is raised up slightly off the pebbled ground and its baked surface protected by a second sheet of non-slip glass. This pathway narrows and broadens out along its length, and curves in plan. A slender ribbon of water follows the line of the path and opens out to create three ponds.

Planting for the scheme is simple: an existing wooded site to the south is retained as a backdrop, while twenty mature larch trees are planted to follow the line of the path. Ivy is also introduced. Underneath the new earth-sheltered banks are spaces to be used as a gallery, a cafe and toilets. Concealed by the landscaping around them, these spaces have all-glass facades – conceived as invisible lenses – providing dramatic views to the castle. The idea for this garden is that it should not be prescriptive. It should instead provide a place for contemplation and pleasure, which is a dramatic new intervention into the historic context of the castle grounds.

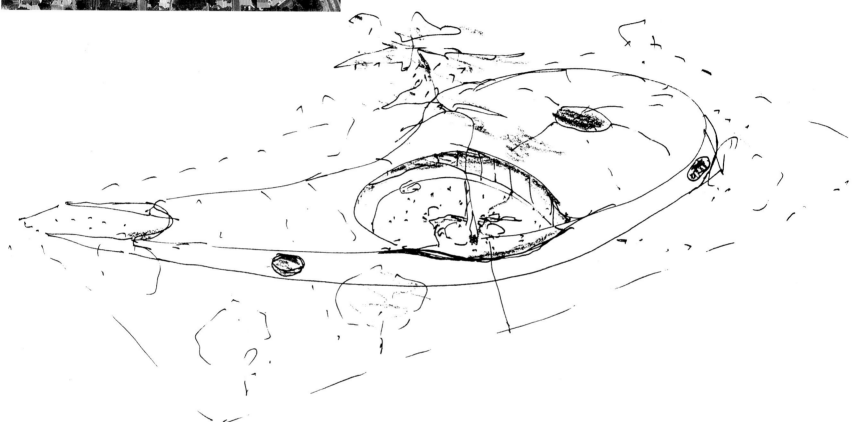

252 MR B HOUSE

1997

This scheme for a modest-sized house in Cambridge is a response to banal suburban surroundings and an attempt to create a fresh and exciting form for the home.

Like the Josef K House (see p74) the proposal is for a simple blockwork structure topped with a semi-monocoque aluminium roof. This roof would be hard-wearing and provide an organic and inspiring volume for the spaces inside. Rather than have conventional windows which overlook surrounding houses, rooflights allow a pleasant top light to filter deep into the plan. Other areas of the house look onto a small courtyard.

Inside, the living space is open plan, with rooms arranged around the perimeter. Walls are lined with insulation and a finish which could be soft, like those at the Media Centre (see p92).

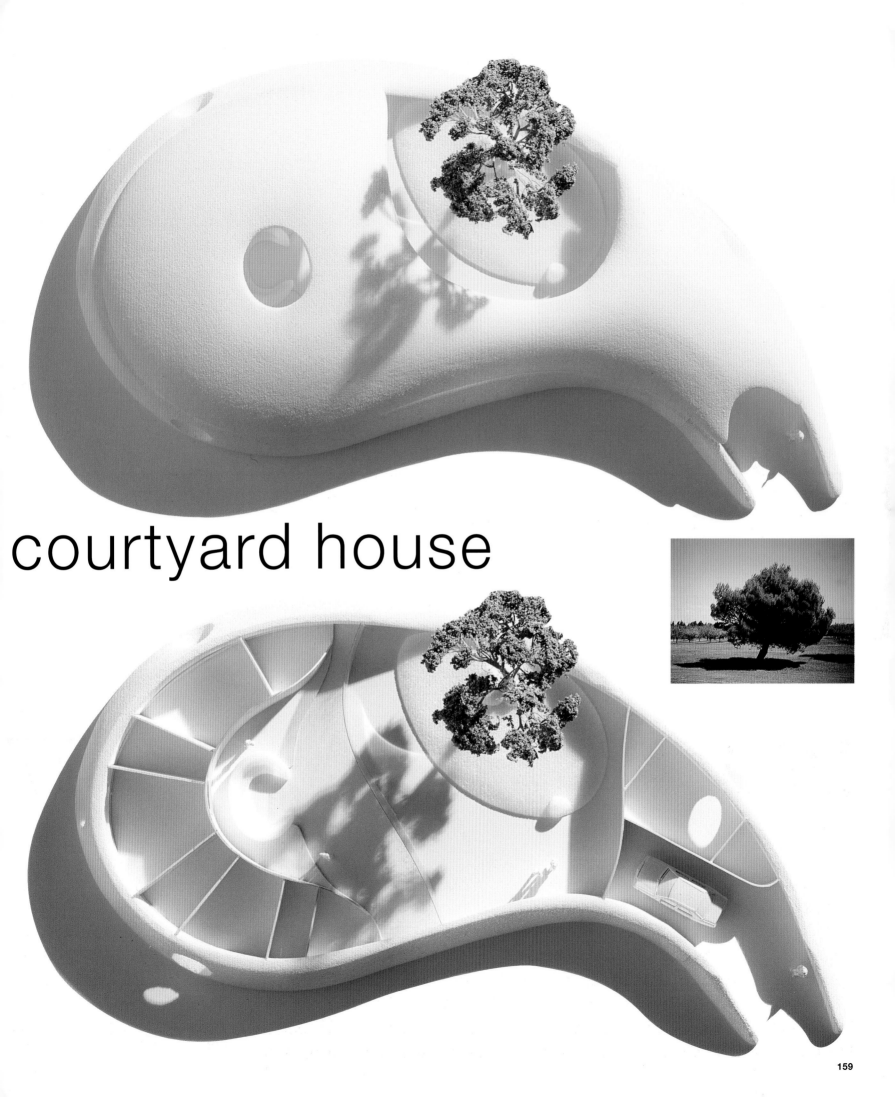

courtyard house

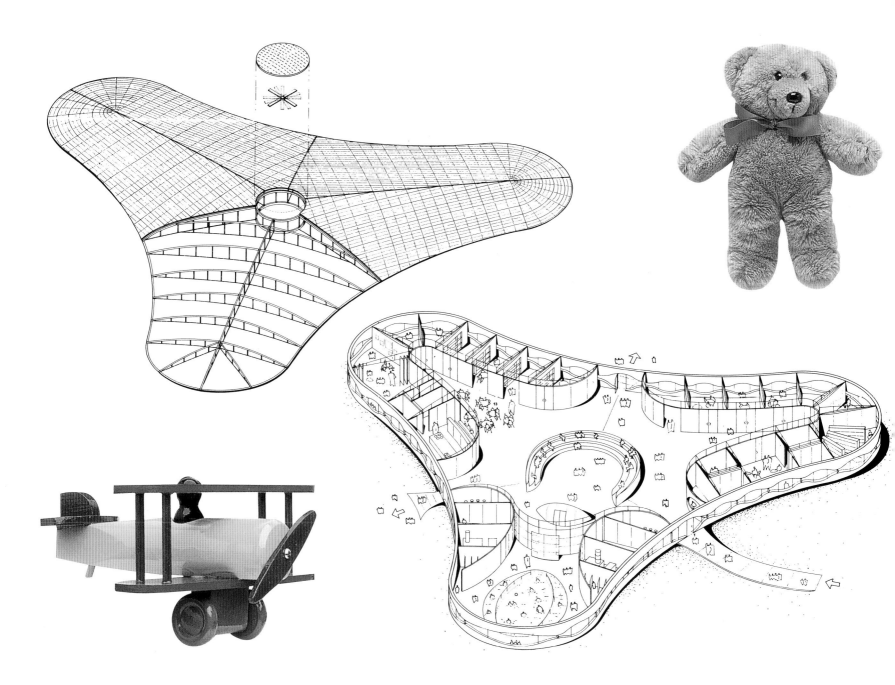

254 BEDFORD SCHOOL 1997

This was an entry for an invited competition to design a new nursery school in Bedford. Drawing on earlier projects for schools, including the Frankfurt Kindergarten of 1990 (see p196) and the Hallfield School project of 1996 (see p142), the architects proposed a single-storey top-lit space to provide maximum daylight throughout. The primary purpose of the windows are to frame views rather than to admit light.

The teaching spaces in the school are arranged around a central meeting area and partitioned by walls which double as service ducts and storage areas. By avoiding the need for corridors, maximum space is given over

360 children

to teaching. As with Hallfield and the Frankfurt Kindergarten, the emphasis is on the quality of the spaces created and the energy-efficiency of the building. A number of options for construction materials are being considered, including aluminium (like the Media Centre), concrete, steel and plywood. The exterior skin of the school could be spray-painted or printed with designs of drawings by children.

Future Systems now intends to explore these ideas further in order to develop a high-quality prototype school which could be prefabricated and mass-produced, like a Portakabin, for use anywhere in the country.

255 COMME DES GARÇONS, NYC 1998

Rei Kawakubo, the Japanese fashion designer who launched the famous Comme des Garçons label in 1973, is celebrated for her innovative approach to the materials and structure of clothes. Such sophisticated garments demand retail environments to match and so Comme des Garçons formed a natural alliance with Future Systems as collaborators and architects for its three most recent shops.

The first, completed in the spring of 1999, is a flagship shop in New York. The site chosen for the project is a run-down looking nineteenth-century industrial building in West Chelsea, an area more associated with contemporary art galleries than fashion shops (the store has relocated from the increasingly commercial SoHo area). Rather than refurbish the entire structure, the approach has been to retain the original exterior – complete with existing fire escapes and signage – and simply to insert a new and intriguing shop behind.

To transport the shopper from the gritty life of the street to the serene and contemplative environment of the interior, Future Systems has devised a shapely 'link' structure which is as innovative in form and materials as Kawakubo's clothes. 'This is a real monocoque structure,' explains Kaplicky, describing how – just like an egg shell – the skin and structure of the tunnel are one. 'There are no ribs or spars and so it is a first in architecture.' The tunnel is made from 6 mm aluminium sheets, cut and assembled to the architect's computer drawings, in the Pendennis boatyard in Cornwall. The hand-sanded finish gives it a crafted appearance, which contrasts with its machine-made aesthetic.

For Future Systems this modest project represents another milestone in the history of the practice. As with the Media Centre at Lords, the structure has been prefabricated in a workshop environment and finished to a high standard before being packed and transported to site. Once there, it was 'grafted' behind the existing brick structure, complete with a pivoting glass door and a row of glowing red light fittings set into the floor.

For Kawakubo meanwhile, the tunnel provides a dramatic interface between her work and the city. 'The concept was to create something hidden, something private,' she says. 'To give the sensation of exploration. A tunnel to take you from one world into the next.'

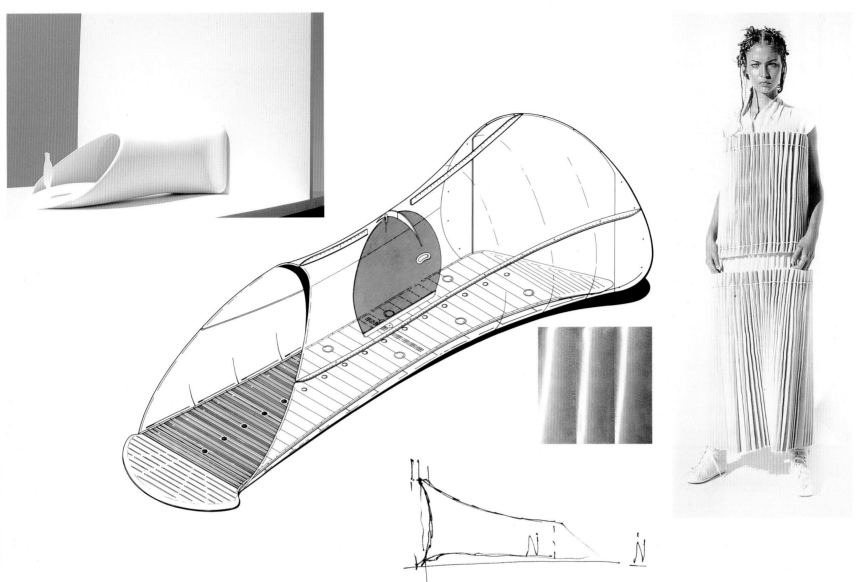

monocoque tunnel

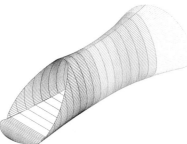

translucency

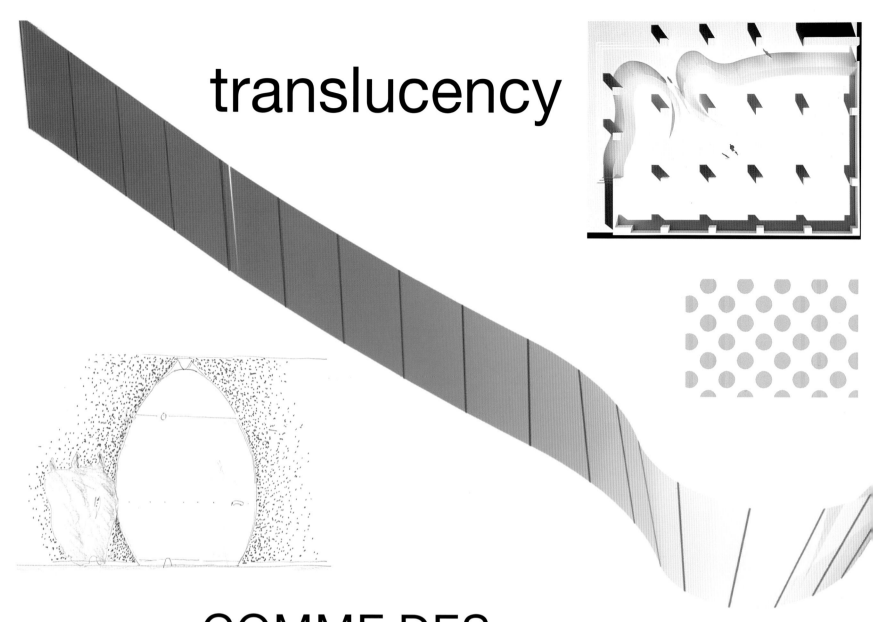

257 COMME DES GARÇONS, TOKYO 1998

As part of an ongoing collaboration between Comme des Garçons and Future Systems, the architects were commissioned to remodel the exterior of their flagship Tokyo store.

To counter the banal building which plays host to the shop, Future Systems developed a scheme for a dramatic glazed facade which lends a softer and unexpectedly organic line to the street corner. Replacing the conventional shop window, this new facade consists of a series of large panels of glass covered with spotted film. These are not only set at a dramatic angle of 18 degrees but many of the panels are also curved. The sensuous snaking line of this window recalls the elegant curved shopfronts of the Modern Movement, both in Kaplicky's home city of Prague and elsewhere. In this updated version however, the brightly coloured film on the glass reflects the rapid movement of the contemporary city. At the same time it challenges the tasteful, but dull, minimalism which has become the clichéd style of high fashion stores the world over.

curved

glass wall

260 COMME DES GARÇONS, PARIS 1999

In the third of a series of designs for Comme des Garçons shops, Future Systems has developed a proposal for a historic site in the centre of Paris to create an outlet dedicated entirely to perfume.

The strategy for dealing with the worn stone facade has been to protect and enhance it with a new 'shield' of delicately coloured glass, an approach already tested in the Wild at Heart flower shop in London (see p148). In Paris the whole facade is covered with a bright blue layer of film sandwiched between two panes of glass. The colour decreases in intensity as it rises up the facade allowing the original stone front to show through. Minimum fixings have been used and the door forms an integral part of the glazing.

Inside, the contrasts continue as a concrete floor is juxtaposed with a curvaceous rear wall in a soft finish normally used for acoustic control. Like the 'blue suede' lining of the Media Centre at Lord's, the effect is reminiscent of a car or aeroplane interior and counters the predictable stone or painted plaster finishes of other fashion stores.

As with Future Systems' display units for Harrods Way-In department (see p190), the cash desk and perfume cabinet here are custom-designed in aluminium. Just like the clear bottles and raw packaging of Comme des Garçons' perfumes, the emphasis is on pure, sensual experience.

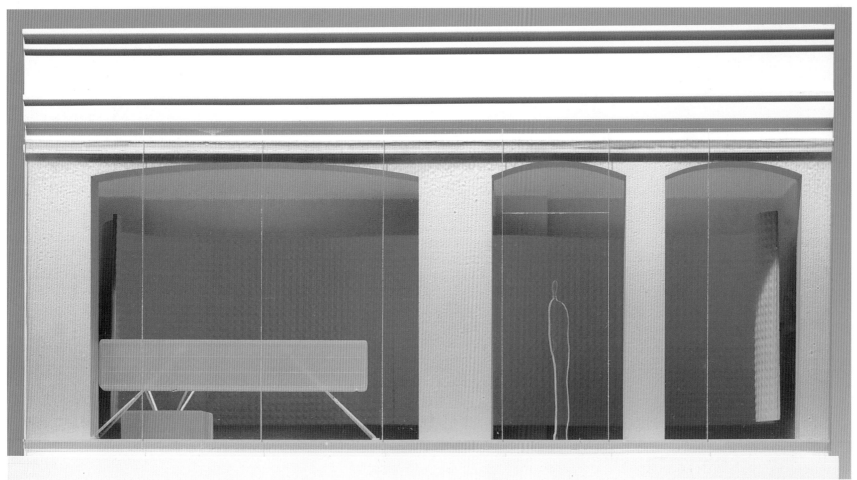

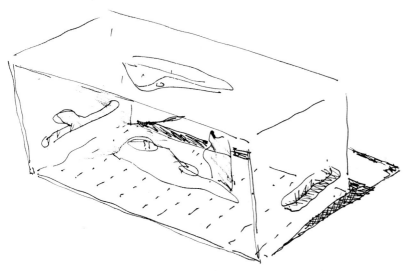

perfume

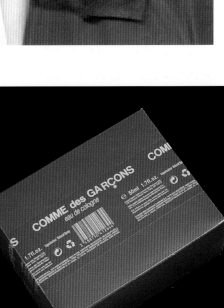

ODEUR 53 EAU DE TOILETTE

COMME DES GARÇONS PARFUMS.A. 16 PLACE VENDÔME
75001 PARIS. INGREDIENTS: ALCOHOL DENAT. (65% VOL.),
AQUA, PARFUM. CONTENTS: SD ALCOHOL 39-C
(65% VOL.), WATER, FRAGRANCE. CET ARTICLE NE PEUT
ÊTRE VENDU QUE PAR LES DÉPOSITAIRES AGRÉES
COMME DES GARÇONS. PRODUCT OF FRANCE.

COMME des GARÇONS

200 ML. 6.8 FL.OZ.

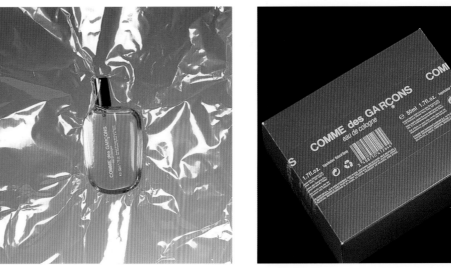

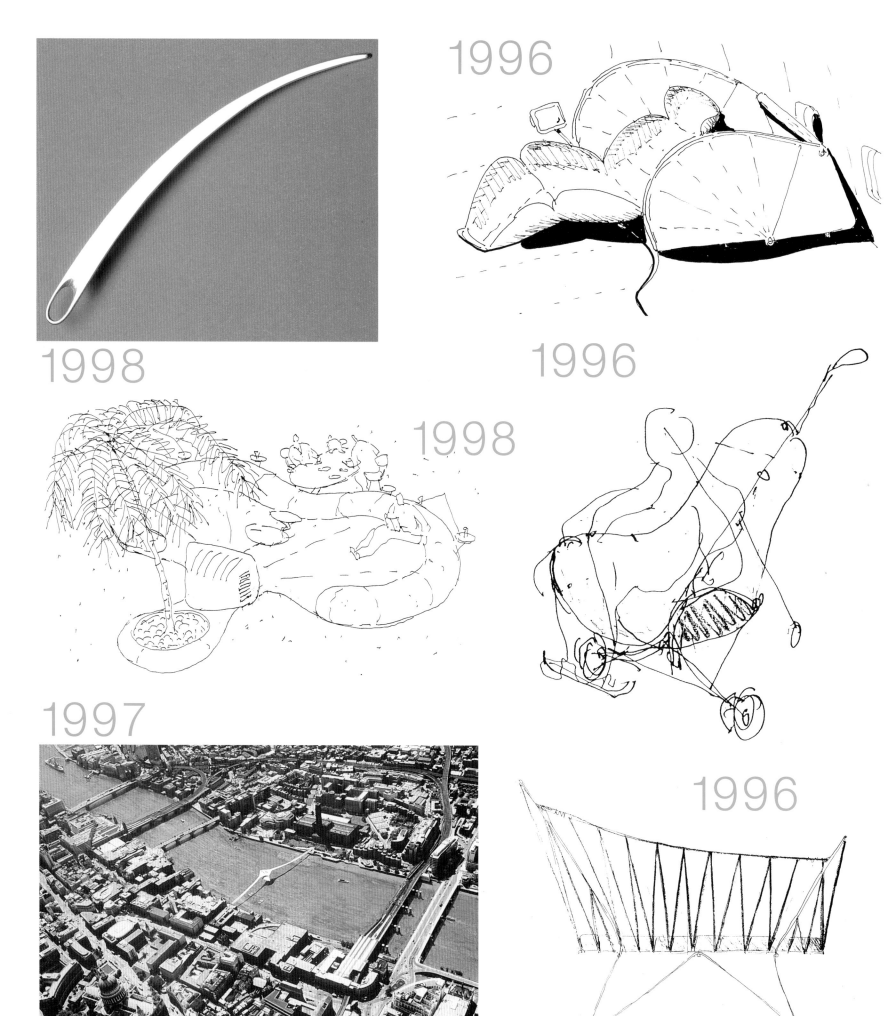

1996

1996

1998

1997

1996

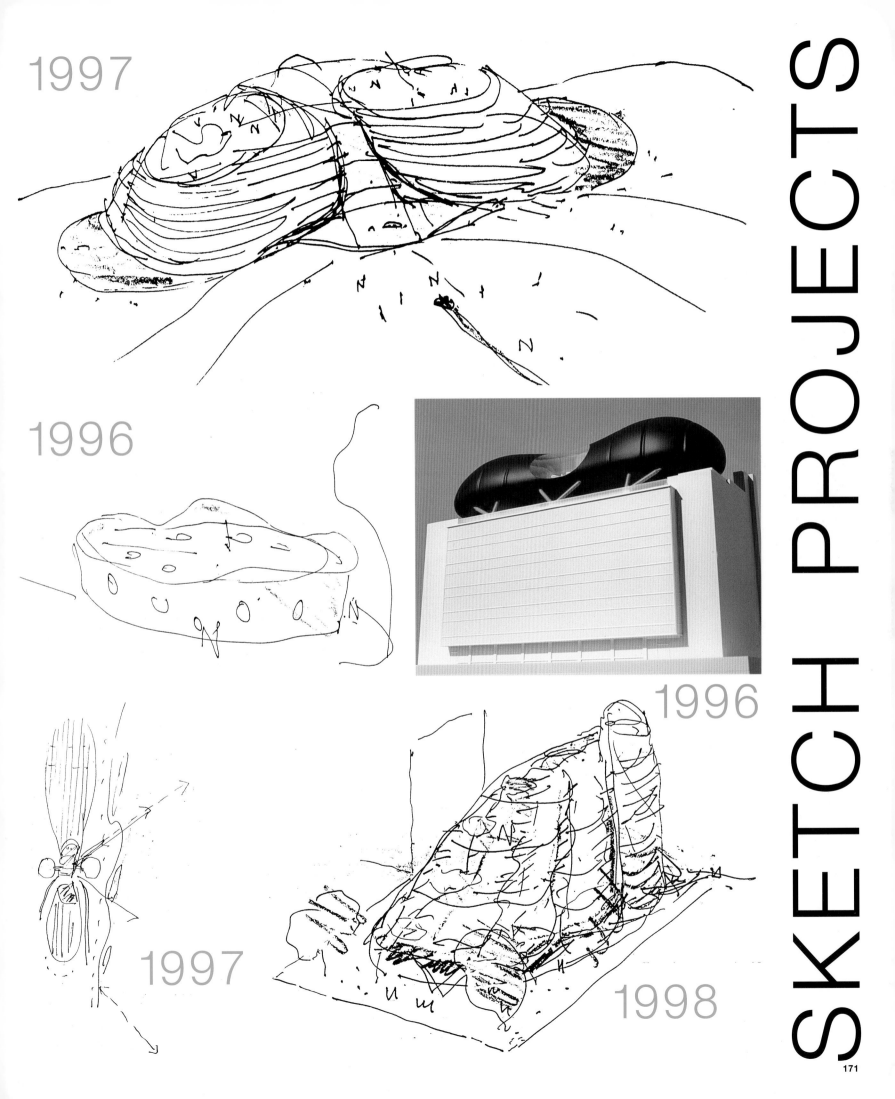

1997

1996

1996

1997

1998

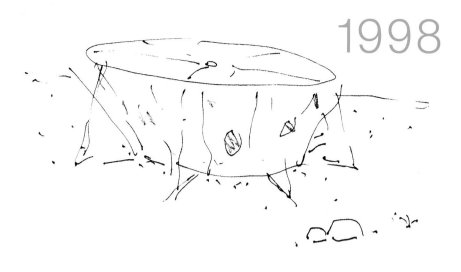

1998

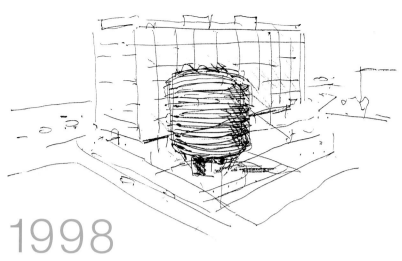

1998

1997

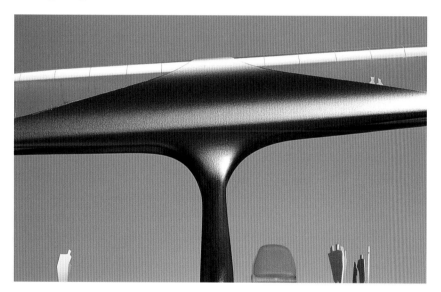

1996

1998

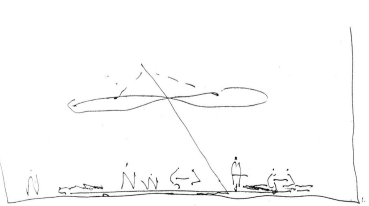

1997

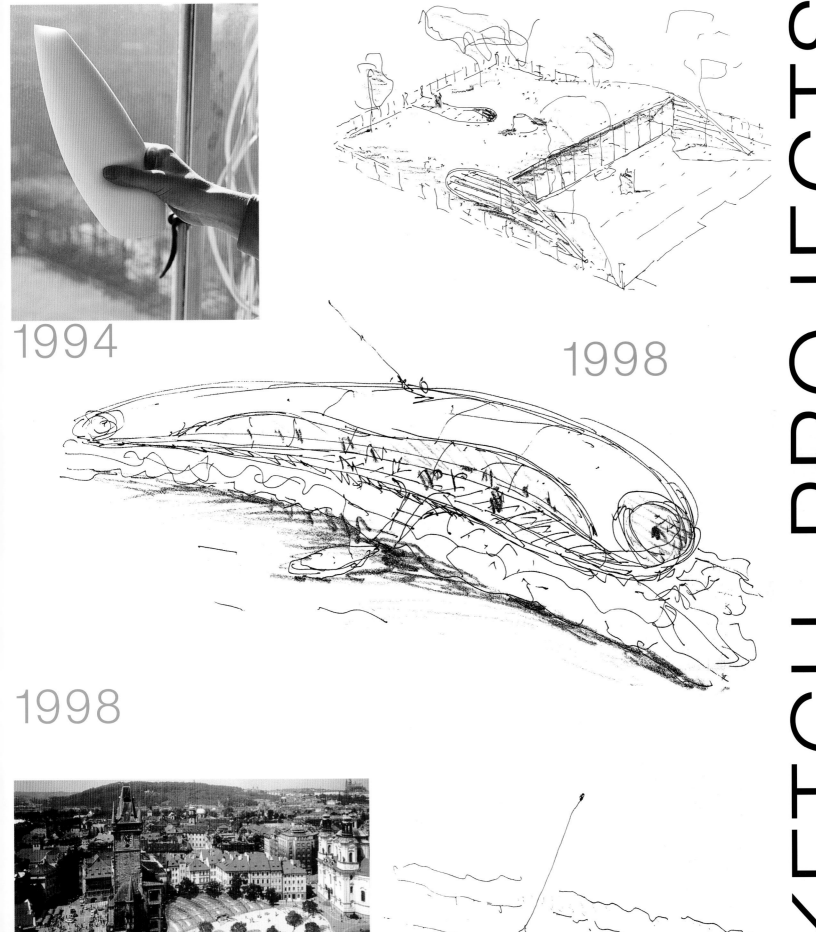

1994

1998

1998

1998

SKETCH PROJECTS

Jan Kaplicky grew up in the Prague suburb of Orechovka, with his father, a sculptor and designer, and his mother, a professional painter of plants and flowers. His early experiences of

FUTURE SYSTEMS:

1937–68

'It all started a long time ago – more than thirty years ago – somewhere in the middle of Europe,' says Jan Kaplicky, introducing a lecture on the work of Future Systems to a group of students in early 1999. Although the architectural practice Future Systems was officially established by Kaplicky and the British architect David Nixon in 1979, and consolidated in a new partnership with Amanda Levete in the late 1980s, its origins can be traced back to Kaplicky's formative years growing up in Czechoslovakia and training and working as an architect under the Communist regime.

Kaplicky was born in 1937 in a suburb of Prague called Orechovka. His father Josef was a respected sculptor, landscape architect and designer of interiors and furniture and his mother Jirina was a professional painter of plants and flowers. His parents were liberal intellectuals whose house was filled with books and publications (including the American magazine *Life*). 'My father was part of the Modern Movement,' says Kaplicky. 'Modern Art was respected in Czechoslovakia far more than in England.' Debate flourished in their house and this atmosphere had a significant effect on the young Kaplicky, as did the surroundings of the family home and city. 'We had some pieces of Corb-inspired furniture and we went to see Plecnik's work at the castle [the renovations carried out by the Slovenian architect between 1920 and 1934],' remembers Kaplicky. 'Maybe they were privileges.'

Growing up in Orechovka, Kaplicky was also exposed to some fine examples of Czech Functionalism, the forward-looking architectural movement – informed by work in France by

modern architecture and design were informed by Czech Functionalist buildings in Prague, his father's architecture books and the military hardware of the British and Americans.

A HISTORY

Le Corbusier and in Germany by the Bauhaus – that developed in the young Republic during the years between the two world wars. Among the most notable examples are the thirty-three villas in the nearby Baba estate built in the early 1930s. Also formative in Kaplicky's early architectural experiences were the radical developments of the same period in the centre of Prague. Even today the elegant glazed front of the Bata shoe store (1929), and the intricately detailed shopping arcades with their glass block vaulted roofs, remain important references for him. The ambition represented by such buildings – to push forward boundaries both in technology and in living conditions – is one which Kaplicky and Levete also share.

The liberal atmosphere and burgeoning cultural scene in the Czechoslovakia of Kaplicky's youth was brought to a sudden halt when the Nazis occupied the country in 1939. His early interest in the technology and form of transport vehicles is revealed by two memories of this period, including the first time he saw an American Universal truck captured by the Germans. 'It was like a mystery object,' he recalls. 'The shape was so different from the German equivalent.' Shortly after, Kaplicky saw an American B17G bomber which had been flown into Prague in 1946 for an air display. The aluminium aeroplane, shown in its glistening, natural state unpainted, had a lasting effect and the metal was later to become one of his favourite materials.

Kaplicky's architectural education at the School of Applied Arts in Prague (1956–62), his two trips to the United States in 1964 and 1966, and his early work in Czechoslovakia, have been well documented by Martin Pawley in his book *Future Systems: The Story of Tomorrow*.

From his earliest days as a student in Prague, Kaplicky was interested in developing an architecture which drew on the technology and processes of industrial production. When the

Despite the restrictions of the Communist regime, Kaplicky's privileges as a student and independent architect allowed him access to news of international developments in design and architecture. 'The library was good,' he recalls. 'There was every magazine, but no books on Czech Functionalism because it was considered bourgeois.'

Kaplicky's frustrations increased, however, when he began working in 1964 from a studio in his mother's house. 'Very little building took place,' he says of the period. There was also the restriction on freedom of ideas and fear of arrest for anybody who overstepped the mark. 'Early on [under the Communist regime] you could meet and discuss things,' remembers Kaplicky, 'but then some friends became part of the new system and so you didn't invite them home anymore.' Despite all this, Kaplicky managed to complete a number of impressive projects, including his first project, a loft conversion, a concrete summer house, a memorial plaque for Franz Kafka's birthplace and the remodelling of a house for the scriptwriter Jaroslav Dietl. Here he designed a ramp in welded steel sections which exercized what Martin Pawley has called a 'daring cantilever'.

In August 1968, with the dramatic invasion of Czechoslovakia by Soviet troops, Kaplicky was forced to make a decision that changed his life. 'We spent the first day resisting, and then we saw it was a hopeless case. I thought, "do I want to be an architect or do I want to try and do something here?"' Kaplicky – like 130,000 other people – obtained an exit visa, burned his personal papers and left his country, escaping on a train and arriving in London in September 1968 with just $100 and the bags he carried with him.

Soviet army invaded in 1968, Kaplicky left Prague for London. He worked for Denys Lasdun and Richard Rogers, in whose office he ran the project for a roof extension in Marylebone.

1968–89

In London Kaplicky's traditional architectural education meant he soon found work with a number of small practices before joining the office of Denys Lasdun where he worked on the National Theatre project until 1971. For him, though, the language of concrete Brutalism was uninspiring and he wanted to move on. 'Thirty years ago this place didn't have an architectural culture,' he recalls of his early days in Britain. 'Everything was still Corb, Banham and the Smithsons. Nobody knew Rogers and Foster in 1968.'

In March 1971, Kaplicky joined the office of Richard Rogers who had recently established his own small practice (Kaplicky became the sixth member of the team). 'I had seen Foster and Rogers' Reliance Controls building in a magazine and I thought "that's Top of the Pops",' remembers Kaplicky. Rogers himself looked at photographs of Kaplicky's Czech work and recognized a kindred spirit. Only two-and-half years after arriving in London, Kaplicky was running the project for a rooftop extension located at the top of building housing Rogers' office in Marylebone. This extension, comprising 'Yellow Submarine'-coloured aluminium sandwich panels on tubular steel portal frames, is a classic piece of Pop architecture. In its elegant, economical form, use of materials and ambition to create a dramatic open-plan space, it also anticipates the work that was to follow. Significantly, it is also the project that introduced Kaplicky to the engineer Anthony Hunt, an important collaborator on later Future Systems projects.

When the Rogers office shifted its attentions to Paris and the project for the competition-

Kaplicky joined the office of Norman Foster in the early 1970s. Kaplicky designed his own London flat to include a conversation pit and advertising images. In the mid-1970s he began a

winning Pompidou Centre, Kaplicky remained in London, living with his partner, the Czech architect Eva Jiricna, and working in the office of Norman Foster. There he worked on the aluminium suspended ceilings for the seminal Willis Faber Dumas office building in Ipswich, a curvaceous and startlingly contemporary solution which Kaplicky still ranks among his most admired buildings.

In 1973 Kaplicky and Jiricna moved into a small flat in the Bayswater area of London. This ordinary apartment was soon transformed into a funky pad, complete with custom-made circular sofa system (a feature which appears, modified, in later Future Systems projects), padded bathroom walls and blow-up images of advertising hoardings which, for Kaplicky and Jiricna, were bold symbols of a free economic and political system. This flat in Archery Steps remained Kaplicky's home for more than twenty years.

Kaplicky's working life during the economically and politically unstable 1970s was somewhat turbulent. After a period of employment with Spence and Webster working on an unbuilt project for a new Parliamentary building, he once again started to develop his own projects. From April 1975, he began in earnest to design speculative schemes, many of them extraordinary and – for most people – futuristic-looking. An important factor in their design, however, was that they always utilized existing technology. The first of these projects, a rural retreat called Cabin 380, is a five-metre long pod which combines Kaplicky's interest in the mass-production technology of cars, planes and boats. This motif of a contemporary home in a wild natural setting is something that appears again and again in

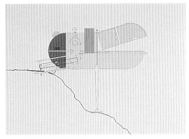

series of visionary schemes, like Cabin 380, which inform later Future Systems projects. In 1977 he rejoined Foster's office where he worked on the Hongkong and Shanghai Bank.

Future Systems' work and one which has finally been realized in the house on the Pembrokeshire coast of Wales (Project 222, see p102).

It was a shared interest in the potential of transferred technologies from industries such as aeroplane, boat and car manufacture to the building industry which drew Kaplicky into a working partnership with the British architect David Nixon. The pair became friends in 1976 while working for Louis de Soissons on a project for Brighton Marina. Kaplicky and Nixon soon began collaborating on speculative schemes and competitions at which they were often successful. Among early wins was a proposal to install a Saturn rocket in the centre of Liverpool and an ideas competition for a Landmark Tower in Melbourne.

In 1977, soon after meeting Nixon, Kaplicky once again joined the office of Norman Foster. By this time Foster's office had grown into a large-scale business with big international projects. Kaplicky was employed there until 1983, working on designs for major buildings, including the Hongkong and Shanghai Bank and the unbuilt scheme for a new BBC Radio headquarters in Portland Place (this reveals many of the low-energy environmental concerns which also became a significant feature and interest in Future Systems' own work). In addition to working on these projects, Kaplicky's talents as a visionary designer and skilled draughtsman ('he draws beautifully,' comments Levete) were put to use in the 'think-tank' division of Foster's office. Here he worked on research, speculative schemes and a project to make new design drawings of all Foster projects undertaken since 1969. During his time at Foster Associates, Kaplicky maintained his working relationship with

In the late 1970s, Kaplicky began working with the architect David Nixon on speculative projects and competitions, many of which were exhibited at the Art-Net gallery. Nixon and Kaplicky

David Nixon, formalizing their partnership in 1979 with the naming of their collaboration as Future Systems. Already their ideas had been recognized as significant in architectural circles, a fact confirmed by the mounting of exhibitions of their work in 1977 and 1978 at the Bloomsbury gallery Art-Net run by Peter Cook (a co-founder of Archigram, the architectural ideas group much admired by Kaplicky). When Nixon moved to California in 1980 to pursue his interests in the architectural application of the technology of space travel, the partnership was maintained by telephone and regular meetings. In the next decade they achieved increased attention as their work became more widely publicized.

In 1987, this body of work was drawn together in an exhibition at the Architectural Association in London (where Kaplicky had been teaching since 1982) which consolidated the pioneering reputation of Future Systems. In the introduction to the catalogue, Kaplicky and Nixon set out their agenda as 'an ideas laboratory to generate design concepts which demonstrate how this inertia [in the building industry] can be overcome by exploring new direction for shaping the future of architecture through revitalized building technology.' Taking as their role models the highly finished products of the marine, aviation and space travel industries, Future Systems declared: 'Architects and engineers and builders have similar responsibilities to ensure that the buildings they design and construct are reliable, efficient and safe for the occupants.' At the same time, Nixon and Kaplicky recognized the potential with this technology to build 'an architecture of sleek surfaces and slender forms – an architecture of efficiency and elegance, even excitement.'

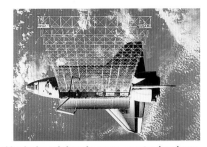

-FUTURE SYSTEMS-

worked together as Future Systems for ten years – with Nixon based in LA – developing radical and influential ideas for structures inspired by industrial and space-age technology.

In this catalogue are some of the key Future Systems projects of the period. All of them display a consistency with these statements. The 1982 project for a new reference and exhibition building at Kew Gardens shows an elegant circular building with an aluminium skin which is informed by manufacturing technology in the aircraft industry. Among the many projects for human habitation in rural settings is the Peanut (1984), a project, for a living pod on the arm of a standard articulated hydraulic crane, which has become iconic in modern architectural history. On a much larger scale is the 150-storey Coexistence tower, an extraordinary research project funded by the Graham Foundation in Chicago which takes as its starting point the need to develop structures for comfortable, sustainable and efficient ways of accommodating people in the modern, densely packed city. The Blob is another such project, speculatively designed for a site in Trafalgar Square and responding in its curvilinear form to London's irregular street plan. This combination of concern for people, politics and the environment, as well as the research and development of architectural ideas, has become increasingly important in Future Systems' work.

Two built projects also featured in the 1987 exhibition. These were the remodelled flat for the design journalist Deyan Sudjic (1983) and the fit-out of the Way-In fashion department at Harrods (1985), a project carried out in collaboration with Eva Jiricna. Although both take the form of interventions into existing spaces, they display Future Systems' declared intention to challenge convention. In the flat all the services are contained in raised floor platforms, an aluminium-lined opening and ramp link the main spaces and all the kitchen

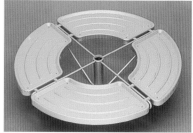

Among early projects realized by Future Systems is the interior of a London flat for Deyan Sudjic and the fashion department at Harrods, both of which borrow from space travel

functions are contained in a single workstation. For the Harrods project the architects developed a flexible system of vacuum-formed aluminium panels for the perimeter walls and over 150 custom-designed mobile display units, also in aluminium. The concept of creating a total environment extended to the matt black finish for walls and ceilings, black granite for the floors and a new graphics treatment for the Way-In logo and packaging. With the combination of sexy space-age shapes and rich colours it is no wonder that the architect Ron Herron was led to describe the work in the show as 'exquisite and mouthwatering'.

The exhibition confirmed Future Systems' position as more than just another gang of High-Tech architects. Here were people with ideas and commitment to the research and development of a truly forward-looking architecture. All that was required now were clients with matching determination to build.

1989–92

Following the 1987 exhibition a number of significant events occurred which changed the practice. These changes were largely the result of Kaplicky's newly-formed relationship with the architect Amanda Levete. The pair had met as early as 1983, but in 1987 they began living and working together. Around this time David Nixon became more involved in projects in the USA and eventually ceased to be involved in Future Systems' work.

Levete was born in Wales in 1955, the daughter of a banker and a ballet dancer. She grew

technology. In the late 1980s Kaplicky began working with Amanda Levete who became a partner in Future Systems. A major show of their work was staged at the RIBA in London.

up in London where she went to St Paul's school and, briefly, art school in Hammersmith before enrolling at the Architectural Association in the early 1970s. After a stint travelling in the USA and working for the practice of Will Alsop, she completed her training at the AA and began working for YRM Architects in 1982. From 1984 until she joined Future Systems full-time in 1989, Levete worked at the Richard Rogers Partnership. For much of her time there she was in charge of the £30 million conversion of the old Billingsgate fish market into a new banking facility, a role in which she gained considerable experience as a project manager.

By 1989, however, with the Billingsgate project complete, Levete was ready to make a move. 'After that there was nothing to move on to of that scale,' she remembers, 'so I decided to set up with Jan.' Having collaborated with Kaplicky on a number of speculative projects while still working for Rogers, she could see the potential in a more formal partnership. So in 1989 she left Rogers' office, Kaplicky gave up his teaching post at the AA (he had been working there since leaving Foster's office in 1983) and the pair set up a central London office together as Future Systems. 'We didn't have a single job,' recalls Levete. 'All we'd done was enter the competition for the Bibiliothèque Nationale.' That move proved to be fortuitous as, in August 1989, Future Systems made it through to the final stage of the competition (between just two schemes) for the French national library, producing an iconic design and earning a useful fee in the process.

Future Systems' memorable scheme for 'a library of parent and child', a vast store of printed words housed in two curved, organic structures (the 'parent') separated by a glazed

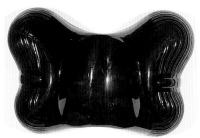

The first project undertaken by Kaplicky and Levete from their new London office was runner-up in a competition for the Bibliothèque Nationale de France. Another early collaboration is a

walkway and zone of electronic information (the 'child'), attracted global attention both in the architectural press and beyond. Although pipped at the post by Dominique Perrault's scheme, Future Systems' entry consolidated and advanced many earlier principles which would continue to be developed in the new partnership of Kaplicky and Levete. Among these are the increasingly organic forms of the buildings (the library is expressed as a wind-sculpted rock formation) combined with a serious concern for energy-efficiency and other 'green' issues.

'When I look back,' says Levete, 'it was probably the happiest time we've had working together because it was very new and exciting. Jan had an international name already and I learnt a lot.' After the excitement of the French library project the pair set about finding work for their new office. Although they undertook a number of significant design projects in the following years, the dire economic recession in Britain between 1990 and 1995 meant that very few of these were built. Unlike many other architectural practices, however, Future Systems survived the slump and achieved some significant projects along the way. Among the major unbuilt ones are the competition entries for a new Museum of the Acropolis in Athens ('that remains one of my favourite projects,' says Levete) and for a visitor centre at Stonehenge, as well as the speculative scheme for a highly influential mixed-use development called the Green Building.

The project for the museum in Athens draws on earlier low-lying Future Systems projects such as the Kew building, but is infused with a new spirit. 'The project would have been very different if I hadn't been involved,' says Levete. 'Jan would never have used glass in that

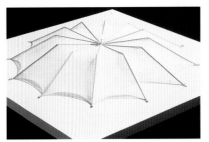

competition entry for a Museum of the Acropolis in Athens. The practice's ambition is to build functional buildings which are spiritually uplifting and challenge conventional forms.

way.' Here there is a sensitivity to the landscape and to the environment as well as the development of a glazed roof structure which features in modified versions in later Future Systems' work, including the 21st Century Gallery and the Ark at the Earth Centre.

Levete brought a fresh eye to Future Systems' body of work and new ideas to add to those which Kaplicky had built up over his twenty years in Britain. 'It was a very closed and introverted world,' she says. 'I think I opened things out. My approach is very much about people using the building, not just the purity of the concept or the form. There's an artistic side to it which doesn't have to be justified in technical terms.'

Looking forward, the partners feel their combined forty years of experience could now be applied to buildings to meet many of the next century's needs. From emergency shelters for the victims of war, famine and homelessness, to housing, schools and places of work, Future Systems have developed ideas for them all.

'There's an obligation for us to keep abreast of what's happening,' says Levete, of the practice's current interests in prefabricated schools, green issues and glass technology. Kaplicky too always keeps a youthful and open mind. 'Maybe the future will be totally different,' he says. 'We've explored Planet Earth, now there's outer space. There will be a permanent space station, a collaboration between Europe, America, Russia and Japan – ten years ago that was unthinkable.' For both of them though, making life better for people is still the ultimate ambition of their work. 'That has to be the motivator,' says Levete. 'The social application is what drives me – touching people is what I would like our work to do.'

PROJECTS

Jan Kaplicky's first executed project was a one-person apartment in the disused roof space of a sixteenth-century building in central Prague. It was a self-build conversion that was completed while Kaplicky was still a student. For furniture he made up copies of Italian canvas-sling chairs, as such items were unobtainable in Prague at the time.

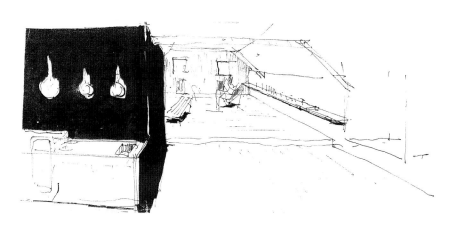

1958   01

ATTIC FLAT

Kaplicky chose components from a concrete panel system intended for high-rise apartments for his second student project. He adapted the standard Czechoslovak system for use in a single-storey house, but the project was never realized. The project, while firmly rooted in the prewar Czech Modern tradition, shows his awareness of the later work of Le Corbusier and the New Brutalists.

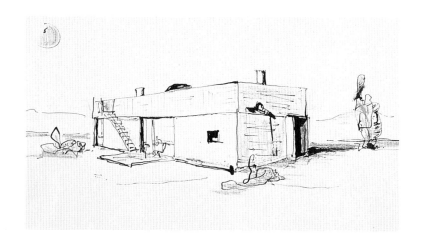

1960   02

CONCRETE HOUSE

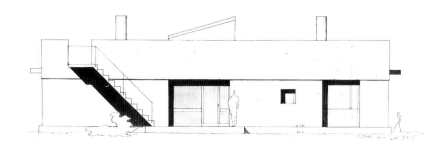

1958–92

Before leaving Czechoslovakia, Kaplicky was to complete an important project for the partially disabled scriptwriter Jaroslav Dietl. He was asked to modernize Dietl's house and garden in Orechovka, with the added requirement that the new mini golf course in the garden be accessible from the first floor living room balcony. For this he designed a slender 10-metre welded-steel ramp, pin-jointed from the garden terrace with a single vertical support. From the support the white-painted ramp is cantilevered 2.4 metres, terminating millimetres from the edge of the balcony.

08 **1965**

JD HOUSE AND GARDEN

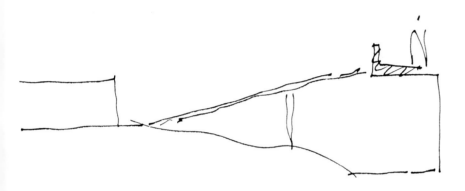

This two-storey family house was built by its owner over a number of years, after Kaplicky left Prague. It is a pragmatic design with strong Miesian plan elements, constructed of rendered brick with a steel-framed flat roof finished with zinc. It was occupied by the original owner for over thirty years.

10 **1967**

FD HOUSE AND STUDIO

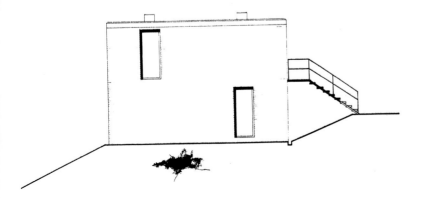

This is an inflatable short-stay accommodation capsule which is capable of being retracted into a secure box when not in use. Its sleeping, bathroom, cooking and storage facilities are supported on an aluminium three-legged structure with retractable trusses and platforms. Inflatable seating and tables are covered over with a transparent inflatable membrane. Anti-sun shields and the orientation of the living pod around its vertical axis allow the user control of the lighting inside. Solar panels provide emergency power.

1980 005

WEEKEND RETREAT FOR MISS B

This interior fit-out of a small apartment in a complex near Hyde Park in London is centred on a raised relaxation pit in the centre of the living space. To one side of this tubular aluminium-framed seating area is a dining area with a cantilevered, perforated dining table, leading through a bulkhead-styled doorway to a recessed kitchen. The wall finishes in the apartment are silver and the floor is black rubber. One wall in the living space is covered with an oversize commercial poster, of the type that stimulated Kaplicky when he first arrived in the West.

1974 017

ARCHERY STEPS

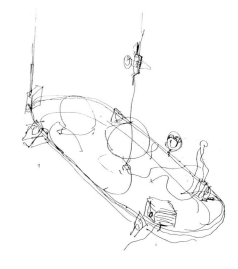

This rural retreat is a kinetic response to living, allowing the inhabitants to control the aspect or orientation of the capsule at any given time. Mounted on a standard articulated hydraulic arm, the two-person unit can be moved between air, ground and water according to mood, activity or time of day, to overcome the fixed viewpoint of static dwellings.

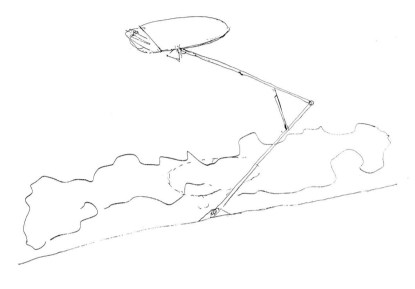

124 **1984**

PEANUT

The improvements to this flat, on the third floor of a nineteenth-century terraced building in North London, aimed to create a series of neutral spacious volumes using innovative design features. The four main spaces, linked by ovoid wall openings that widen at waist level, use office-type raised floors and tensile fabric ceilings to transform the original rooms. The insertion of self-contained units, such as a freestanding kitchen work-unit incorporating all culinary facilities, a raised bed platform and a aluminium-panelled bathroom unit with mounted sanitary fittings, add to the sense of space in this apartment.

118 **1983**

DS FLAT

In association with Jiricna-Kerr Architects, Future Systems developed a new look for 'Way-In' on the fourth floor at Harrods, Knightsbridge. Movable vacuum-formed aluminium panels and standing frames make up the new perimeter walls to separate the main customer areas from changing and stock rooms. Over 150 custom-designed freestanding units, sprayed with silver metallic paint, with interchangeable shelves, rails, mirrors, tables and low-voltage lighting were created for the display of merchandise. The black painted walls and durable black granite flooring provide a neutral background against which the silver elements stand out. The new shop logo, carrier bags, restaurant menu, packaging and photographic murals were also treated as integral parts of the design.

1984 133

'WAY-IN', HARRODS

The Blob, originally designed for a competition but not submitted, is a proposal for the Grand Buildings site at Trafalgar Square, London. The curvilinear shape of the building is generated by the site and the low light intensity caused by the neighbouring buildings. The building focuses on a central atrium, lit by a curved glazed roof and a solar reflector above. The structure of the building is a three-dimensional, internally stiffened dual skin which encloses the building from the roof deck to the street edge. The roof deck is a deep truss from which alternate floors are suspended by hangers. Large circular windows, set into deep reveals, perforate the white ceramic-tiled surface, and allow users contact with outside.

1985 135

BLOB

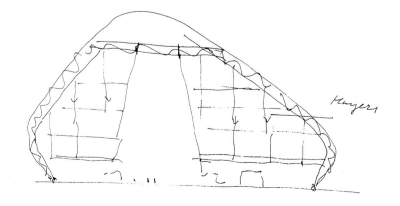

This portable, low-cost, large-span structure was developed for emergency or disaster relief. Like a large umbrella with twelve radial ribs, it can be easily erected by twelve people to shelter up to 200 people, providing storage and distribution areas for food and medicine. Each of the ribs is anchored by sand bags or anchors to withstand wind speeds of up to 130 km/h. The white outer surface of the cover membrane reflects up to 80 per cent of surface radiation and the metallized inner surface maintains heat for the night. When collapsed, its lightweight steel members and membrane can be stowed compactly as one element for air or road transport.

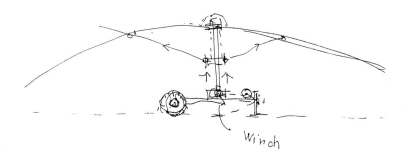

139 **1985**

SHELTER

The octagonal wardroom table has to be easily used in zerogravity and seat up to eight crew members for meetings, meals and working. The table is designed to adapt individually, as work surfaces are unfolded, rotated, angled and adjusted to fit ergonomic and operational requirements. In addition to providing flexibility to its arrangements the table is also designed with task lighting, object restraints, handholds and control panels.

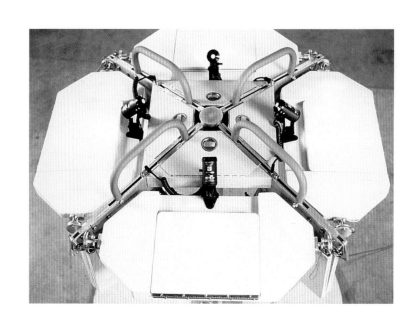

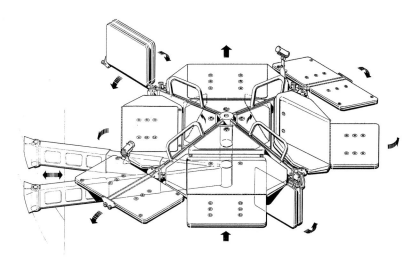

144 **1986**

NASA WARDROOM TABLE

Drop is a self-supporting temporary dwelling for two people. Designed for the 1989 Biennale in Nagoya, it is installed as a complete unit with minimal site preparation, to provide maximum comfort in a confined space. The simple construction is of two semi-monocoque shells composed of a series of ribs and spars welded to the skin, with foam insulation pumped in between. There is a large openable canopy of electro-photochromatic glass, shaded by external horizontal louvres, and incoming air is conditioned in a simple duct/slot system by an air-cooled reversible heat pump, discharged through the floor and over the canopy surface.

1988   165

DROP

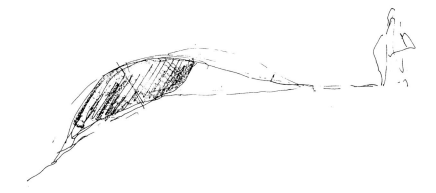

Green Building is a conceptual examination of alternative strategies for a 'green' office environment. The building rests on a tripod megastructure, leaving the ground level to be used as a garden. Each of the hollow steel floor decks are suspended from the apex of the tripod by ties along their internal and external edges. Props and ties support the external and internal skin at floor level, while allowing a natural ventilation space between. The streamlined form draws air over the building surface and wind-scoops direct falling cool air through air intakes into the building. Stale air is vented through louvres at the top and heat is recovered during cooler months. With a fully glazed outer skin, most of the office areas can be lit naturally. Daylight is bounced into the centre of the building by mirrors while light deflectors scatter the sun's rays.

1990   166

GREEN BUILDING

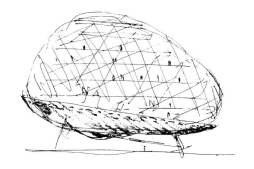

Although Future System's scheme for the invited competition to design the French national library was placed second, it was likened by the assessors to 'a door opening upon the future'. Its design was quite unlike that of any other entrant: a smooth enveloping aerodynamic form, split in two by a vast central glazed valley penetrated by a pedestrian bridge. Four functional accommodation lobes, two on each side of the central axis, provide the reading rooms and research areas of the brief, while the immense collection of books is housed radially in underground levels. Earth excavated from the basement levels is used to raise the levels of a park surrounding the building. The thermal inertia below ground creates a stable environment to store books and fragile documents.

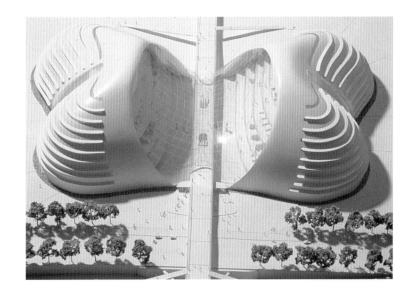

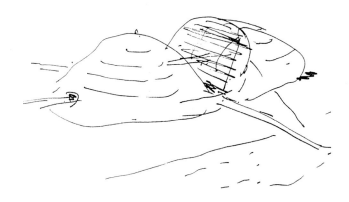

171   **1989**

BIBLIOTHÈQUE NATIONALE DE FRANCE

Although unsuccessful at the competition stage, this design for the Museum of the Acropolis attracted media attention for its unique approach to the site. The body of the museum is sited on the the north slope of Philopappos hill across from the Acropolis and connects to the historic monument by means of a slender, pedestrian cable-suspension bridge spanning the 180 metres across the valley. The museum itself is a large, low, transparent, single-span shell structure, supported at its rim by a compression ring beam. The enclosed area is large enough to support a full-scale model of the footprint of the Parthenon, enabling fragmentary exhibits to be closely related to their source. A cooling system incorporates air ducts cut deep into the rock and shading is provided by alternate zones of solid, perforated and clear panels.

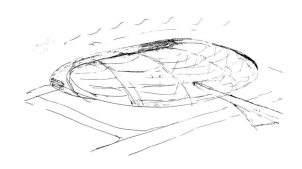

172   **1989**

MUSEUM OF THE ACROPOLIS

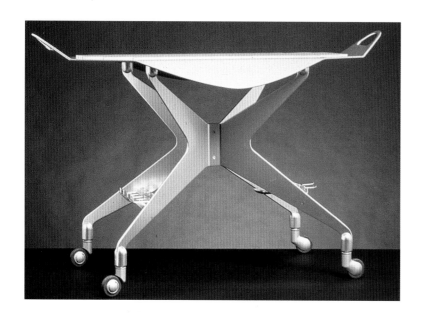

Part of the experience of dining out is the style in which food is served. Filleting at a table can be highly theatrical and the trolley for serving Chateaubriand, Dover sole and lobster should reflect this and yet be functional. The Ivy Trolley is easily manoeuvrable within tight spaces, and is streamlined to emphasize the serving plate. Unlike traditional trolleys it has no lower shelf; instead cutlery is suspended between the legs, and chromed plastic ribs prevent plates from rattling. All of the elements are cut from 6 mm aluminium sheet and bolted together.

1990 178

IVY TROLLEY

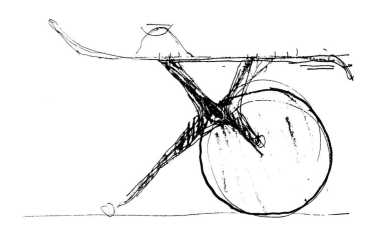

Chiswick Business Park is a complex of offices and leisure facilities set in landscaped grounds in West London. The entrance gateway – a bird-like structure – is intended to encourage people to stroll into the gardens. The smooth aerodynamic form, which will cast strong shadows over the entrance, is a double cantilever of semi-monocoque aluminium construction, using technology from the boat-building industries. Three prefabricated sections, welded together on site, make up the structure.

1990 182

CHISWICK PARK ENTRANCE

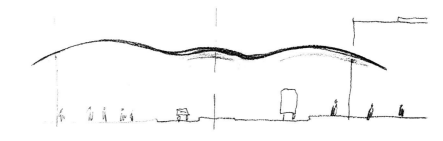

This family house in a suburb of London achieved a number of goals in its construction. Grassed berms on the flanking walls minimize the profile of the single-storey, two-bedroom dwelling and make it less visible from the street. The site was richly planted, yet all existing trees on the site were retained. The house takes advantage of both the south aspect and gentle slope of the site to orient the glazed living space and terrace to the south, and the food preparation area at the central location where the floor level changes. High-level glazing allows south light through partitions to the north-facing bedrooms and bathroom to the rear. The profiled steel roof deck is supported by the cross walls and two exposed cable-stiffened steel trusses running from front to back.

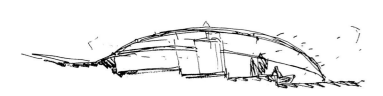

183   **1990**

HOUSE AT BERKHAMSTED

The MOMI hospitality tent is not site-specific but been erected on a site near the National Film Theatre on the South Bank. The architects and engineers envisaged a lightweight, yet dramatic structure for repeated use; six people can erect and dismantle it over two days. The tent has a raised floor assembly of aluminium panels, concealing the electrical services, that rest on steel beams levelled by jacks. Its white Tenara fabric membrane is stretched between pairs of inclined arches formed with 32 mm grp rods, with a braced inclined arch at either end attached to a steel floor-edge beam for stability. The ribs are stabilized with steel struts and tension cables.

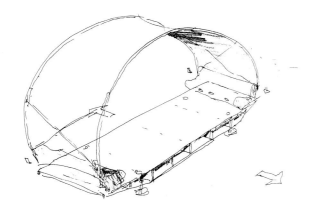

184   **1991**

MOMI TENT

This prototype was one of five winning entries to a competition run by the Museum of Contemporary Art, Sydney. It is a re-evaluation of the caravan in contemporary Australian life, and is reminiscent of the ideals represented by the Airstream caravans of the 1940s. Like a snail, the aerodynamic and lightweight 22 mm semi-monocoque shell wraps over the car body, increasing the wheelbase but decreasing the overall length, thus achieving a low drag co-efficient, fuel efficiency and a small turning circle. Solar panels generate electricity to service the caravan.

1991   186

CARAVAN

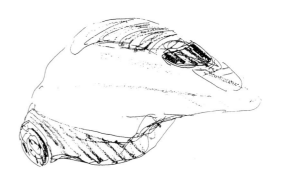

This kindergarten for 100 children between the ages of 3 and 12 is designed to encourage children's understanding of the weather's influence on their environment. The free-form building that emerges from the landscape is covered by a glazed skin which is oriented to make full use of solar energy, incorporating innovative systems for natural ventilation, lighting and heat recovery which enable the building to function efficiently and effectively. Classrooms are clustered around a central space, which provides a top-lit covered area for play, gatherings and assembly. During summer months the classrooms open onto this space to allow cross-ventilation, and in colder weather, fabric screens can be closed. Warm or cold air can be circulated under the floor to moderate the temperature in the classrooms.

1991   190

FRANKFURT KINDERGARTEN

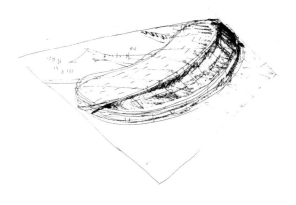

Set in a landscaped park, the building is a competition entry for a 'green' headquarters for the environmental department of the City of Hamburg. The aerodynamic building envelope makes a dramatic addition to the run-down Altona district. Its form resembles that of an open leaf supported by an inclined arch. A transparent south-facing net of glass stretched over the structure incorporates coloured glass by the artist Brian Clarke. A central atrium behind is the focus of movement and activity in the building. Its shape, energy systems and transparency combine to cut down operating demands and reduce polluting emissions to minimal levels.

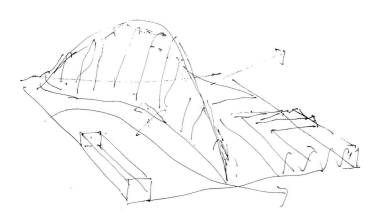

192   **1991**

UMWELTSCHUTZBEHÖRDE HAMBURG

Visitors to Stonehenge can no longer appreciate the ancient monument with the freedom of previous centuries. Time and the pilgrimage of millions have eroded the sacred site which is today sandwiched between two major roads. Future Systems' competition entry connects a low-lying lens-shaped building to the monument by way of a raised metal mesh path across the grassy chalk landscape. The Visitors' Centre, a minimal low-profile insertion into the landscape, is a respectful gathering place, which shelters the movements of arrival and departure from the view of the monument.

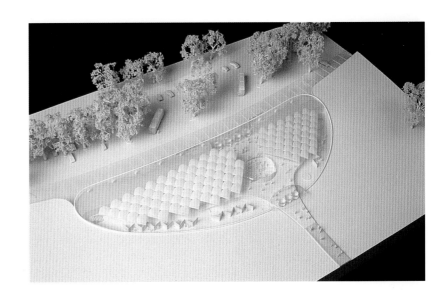

201   **1992**

STONEHENGE VISITORS' CENTRE

PUBLIC + PRIVATE

THE IVY

WEDNESDAY 2ND JUNE, 1993

DRESSED CORNISH CRAB
WITH CELERIAC RÉMOULADE

SERVED WITH GRANARY TOAST

RUMP AND BEST END OF WELSH LAMB
WITH MINTED JERSEY ROYALS
AND NICOISE FRENCH BEANS

"THANK YOU CAKE"

COFFEE OR TEA

WINES

MACON-FUISSÉ 1990 DOMAINE LUCIEN VESSIGAUD
CHÂTEAU HAUT PLANTEY 1987 GRAND CRU ST EMILION

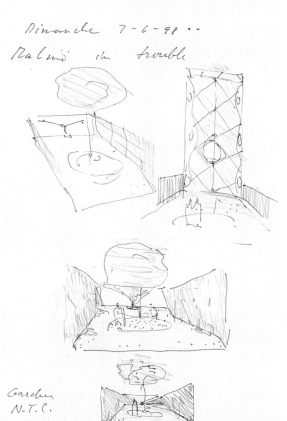

PLICKY

UCLA
SCHOOL OF ARCHITECTURE
& URBAN PLANNING
CORDIALLY INVITES YOU TO:

OPENING · EXHIBIT ·
FUTURE SYSTEMS

PRESS RELEASE
ARCHITECTURAL ASSOCIATION
SCHOOL OF ARCHITECTURE
34-36 Bedford Square, London WC1B 3ES   Telephone 01.636 0974

Future Systems 15 January – 14 February 1987 Ground-floor Exhibition Gallery

ARCHITECTURE INTERNATIONAL SERIES 1992

Future Systems (UK)
Jan Kaplicky and Amanda Levete

Melbourne Lecture Friday, 20 March 1992
Sydney Lecture Tuesday, 17 March 1992

Melbourne Lecture
Coffee 6.00pm Lecture 6.30pm
Shell Theatre, Shell Building
Cnr Flinders and Spring Streets

WOHNBAU
MONTAGE
Mo, 15.11.1993, 18.00

Jan
Kaplicky
FUTURE SYSTEMS

Vortrag - Gr. Aktsaal
TU Wien, Karlsplatz 13
Danach Diskussion im
Institut für Wohnbau

The British Council StadtWien 24
MAGISTRATSABTEILUNG

FUTURE SYSTEMS *Projects by Jan Kaplicky and David Nixon*
School of Architecture Rice University 7 September – 10 October 1988

Future Systems

architecte

jeudi 21 mai 1992 à 19h00   salle de conférences

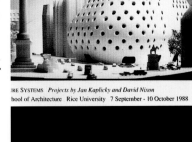

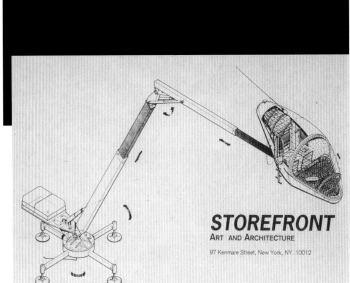

STOREFRONT
ART AND ARCHITECTURE
97 Kenmare Street, New York, NY. 10012

LECTURES

Bartlett School of Architecture, London	1999
Royal Academy of Arts, London	1999
University of Technology, Vienna	1998
IIT, Chicago	1998
Rice University, Houston	1998
University of Portsmouth	1998
ICA Exhibition Talk, London	1998
Architectural Association, London	1998
Technische Hochschule, Darmstaat	1998
The British Constructional Steelwork Association Conference	1997
Women in Marketing	1997
Architekturforum de l'architecture, Biel	1997
Architectural Association, London	1997
ICA – 'Spaced Out' talk, London	1996
5th Architectural Forum, Prague	1996
Architecture Association of Ireland, Dublin	1996
Architecture Foundation, London	1996
ICA – 'Spaced Out' Talk, London	1996
Brussels School of Architecture, Brussels	1996
University of Humberside	1996
Bartlett School of Architecture, London	1995
Association O, Stockholm	1995
Brno Technical University	1995
Royal College of Art, London	1995
Technical University, Prague	1995
University of Manchester	1994
Mackintosh School of Architecture, Glasgow	1994
Royal Institute of British Architects, London	1994
Svenska Arkitekters Riksforbund, Stockholm	1994
Bournemouth & Poole College of Art and Design	1994
Cambridge University	1993
Technische Universitat, Vienna	1993
Cardiff University	1993
Nottingham University	1993
Technische Universitat, Munich	1993
Arc en Rêve Centre d'Architecture, Bordeaux	1992
Technische Universitat, Berlin	1992
International Series – Sydney, Melbourne, Perth	1992
Royal Academy, Copenhagen	1992
Aarhus School of Architecture, Denmark	1992
North Wales Society of Architects	1992
University of Wales, University of Sheffield	1992
Pratt Institute, New York	1992
Scott Sutherland School of Architecture, Aberdeen	1992
Ove Arup & Partners	1992
Polytechnic of East London	1991
Bartlett School of Architecture, London	1991
Birmingham Polytechnic	1991
Chesterfield Arts Centre	1991
Architectural Association, London	1991
Hochschule für Kunste, Bremen	1990
Obec Architektu, Prague	1990
Hogeschool voor de Kunsten, Amsterdam	1990
Technische Hochscule, Aachen	1990
Cambridge University	1990
Oxford Polytechnic	1990

62 LECTURES 1984–2000

PUBLIC + PRIVATE

INVITATIONS

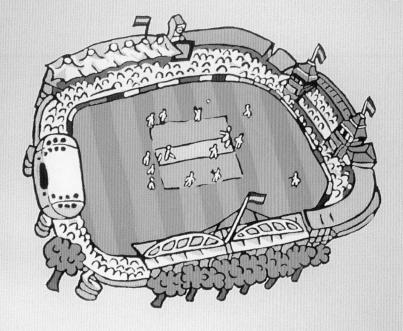

The House of Commons to Lords by bus and Tube?

For your best rout...

call London Trav...

0171 22...

Making Lo...

UNIVERSITY ✠ OF OXFORD

*The Chancellor
requests the pleasure of your company
at the conferment of the degree of DCL upon
His Excellency The President of the Czech Republic
on Thursday, 22nd October 1998 at 12.10 pm
in Convocation House
and afterwards at a Reception
in the Divinity School.*

RSVP by Friday, 16th October: *Academic dress*
The Vice-Chancellor's Secretary
University Offices   *Please be seated by 12.00 noon*
Wellington Square, OX1 2JD
[alison.miles@admin.ox.ac.uk]

THE TIMES TUESDAY DECEMBER 1 1998   4M   9

MP defends clifftop bunker from critics

By SIMON DE BRUXELLES

PLANNERS have been accused of favouritism after allowing a millionaire Labour MP to construct a futuristic holiday home in a national park.

The house is built into a clifftop in Pembrokeshire with stunning views out to sea through its full-length panoramic window.

Bob Marshall-Andrews, the MP for Medway, in Kent, was able to get around restrictions on new development in the national park because his holiday home is built on the site of a primitive wooden chalet.

Barriers that hid construction of the house-like building from walkers using the Pembrokeshire coastal path were removed earlier this month. The unusual design has provoked mixed reactions.

The structure has been turfed over, leading to suggestions by some local residents that it would be more suitable for the Teletubbies than an eminent QC.

Others are unhappy that the MP was able to get planning permissions for a new house when many of them have been unable to make alterations to their properties.

Anne Kenyon, who lives in the village of Nolton Haven and owns holiday homes in the area, said: "It can be a major battle to get an extension or a conservatory but this MP manages to get permission for this terrible eyesore. I cannot understand why planning permission was given for something so out of character." The single-storey house, built into the top of an 80ft cliff at Druidston, has spectacular views of St Bride's Bay through the 60ft long window running the length of its seaward side. The

house, which is believed to have cost about £350,000, has two bedrooms, a lounge with open log fire and a kitchen and two bathrooms designed with in metal pods.

Much of the building was put together in London then taken by road to Pembrokeshire to be buried in the hillside. It was then covered with local turf and planted with gorse in an attempt to help it to blend in. There is no garden and the boundaries of the property have deliberately been left undefined.

Mr Marshall-Andrews, 54, and his wife, Gill, built the property as a holiday home but may retire there. He said

"Reaction from neighbours has been extremely positive. I am very pleased with the design and it has conformed to everything I want. I think it is something brilliant for the future."

But one local businessman, who did not want to be named, said: "It's an ugly blot on the landscape, like something from Star Trek or Teletubbies."

Mr and Mrs Marshall-Andrews, who have two grown-up children, have holidayed in West Wales for the past 25 years. The building was designed by a Czech architect, Jan Kaplicky, of Future Systems in London. It has been featured in the Architects' Journal as an example of how to build in an environmentally sensitive area.

The house also has local supporters, led by Jane Bell, who runs the Druidston Hotel nearby. She said: "It's a very unusual, exciting design and has brought a breath of fresh air to the coastline. It is lovely inside and, once the vegetation has grown back, it will blend in with the surroundings."

The National Park Authority recently provoked criticism after ordering the demolition of experimental environmentally friendly, low-impact homes at an "eco-village" near Newport. Unlike Mr Marshall-Andrews' home, those at Brithdir Mawr have been built using only local materials and are self-sufficient.

Wruth Williams, a spokeswoman for the national park, denied yesterday that the planning committee had been more sympathetic to the development because it was proposed by a well-heeled MP.

"Being an MP did not help him get planning permission. The same rules apply to everyone. It went through the planning process very smoothly and I am not aware there were any objections at all. It is actu-ally a replacement for an old wooden dwelling and planning committee members welcomed the idea of something so innovative.

"It still looks quite bare because quite a lot of landscaping has still to be done. We will be keeping in close contact with Mr Marshall-Andrews to make sure that this is carried out."

The futuristic home built into a Pembrokeshire cliff by Bob Marshall-Andrews, right

201

BIBLIOGRAPHY

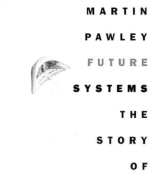

MARTIN
PAWLEY
FUTURE
SYSTEMS
THE
STORY
OF
TOMORROW

PHAIDON

BOOKS

More For Inspiration Only,
Jan Kaplicky, Academy Editions   1999
Hauer–King House Future Systems,
Martin Pawley, Phaidon   1997
For Inspiration Only,
Jan Kaplicky, Academy Editions   1996
The Story of Tomorrow Future Systems,
Martin Pawley, Phaidon   1993
Future Systems,
Architectural Association   1987

A + U	JAP	The Guardian	UK
AA Files	UK	Harpers	UK
Actuel	F	House and Garden	UK
Ambiente	D	ID Magazine	US
Arca	I	ID	UK
Arch+	D	Impact	UK
Archicrée	F	The Independent	UK
Architects' Journal	UK	Insight	UK
Architectural Design	UK	Interni	I
Architectural Record	US	Japan Architect	JAP
Architectural Review	UK	Metropolis	US
Architecture	US	MF DNES	CZ
Architecture Today	UK	Modern Painters	UK
Architecture + Wohnen	D	Moniteur	F
Architecture d'Aujourd'hui	F	Monument	AUS
Architekt	CZ	nest	US
Architektur	A	New Office Age	JAP
Architektura Murator	POL	New Scientist	UK
Arquitectura Viva	ES	The New Statesman	UK
Arena	UK	The New York Times	US
Axis	JAP	Object	AUS
Bauwelt	D	Observer	UK
Big Issue	UK	Omega	AUS
Blitz	UK	Patek	CZ
Blueprint	UK	Perspecta 29	US
Building	UK	Playboy	D
Building Design	UK	Progressive Architecture	US
Construction News	UK	Public: Art: Space	UK
Czech Airlines	CZ	RIBA Journal	UK
De Architect	D	SD	JAP
Detail	D	Storefront Report	US
Design Report	D	The Sunday Telegraph	UK
Design Week	UK	Techniques &	
Designers Workshop	JAP	Architecture	F
Deutsche Bauzeitschrift	D	The Telegraph	UK
Deutsche Bauzeitung	D	Time Out	UK
Die Welt	D	Time	US
Domus	I	The Times	UK
El País	COL	Viz	UK
Elle Decoration	UK	Village Voice	US
Esquire	UK	Vogue	UK
The European	UK	*wallpaper	UK
Evening Standard	UK	Wired	US
The Face	UK	World Architecture	UK
Financial Times	UK	Xantypa	CZ
FX	UK	Zlaty Rez	CZ

90 MAGAZINES + 32 COVERS

Select bibliography

Blueprint 'Comme des aliens'	Feb 1999
Architectural Design 'Des-Res Architecture'	Jan 1999
Architekt 'Jan Kaplicky' Prodejna Kvetin	Jan 1999
Zlaty Rez Future Systems Exhibition Catalogue	Dec 1998
Nest 'Josef and his Amazing Technicolour Dream House'	Dec 1998
'La Collection d'Architecture du Centre George Pompidou'	Nov 1998
Building 'On Site; The Natwest Media Centre'	2 Oct 1998
L'architecture d'Aujourd'hui 'Projet Recents'	Sept 1998
'Future Systems' ICA Exhibition catalogue	April 1998
The Independent 'Beauty and the Beach'	31 March 1998
Architects' Journal 'Future Systems on Show'	26 Mar 1998
Blueprint 'Cool or Quaint? The architecture of Future Systems'	Mar 1998
RIBA Journal 'The Future is Pink'	Mar 1998
Architectural Review 'Wild Bunch'	Mar 1998
Martin Centre Report	1998
'Cities for the Future – Towards New Urban Living'	1997
Architect's Journal 'Artists of the Floating Bridge'	7 Nov 1996
Bauwelt 'Einfamilienhaus in Islington'	18 Oct 1996
Portable Architecture, Robert Kronenburg, Architecture Press	1996
'Renewable Energy Development' European Conference, Venice	1996
'Living Bridges', Royal Academy Catalogue	1996
Blueprint 'London Bridges'	1996
Detail 'Wohnhaus in London'	Feb 1995
L'Arca 'La Finestra sul Cortile'	Jan 1995
Vogue 'The Glass Menagerie'	Oct 1994
The Observer 'Artists of the Floating World'	21 Aug 1994
The Face 'Twenty First Century Vacations'	May 1993
L'Arca 'L'high-pop-ground'	Mar 1993
Detail 'Temporary Structure in London'	Feb 1993
L'Arca 'Il Virtuosismo dell'Ingegneria'	Sep 1992

PUBLICATIONS

FUTURE SYSTEMS

FUTURE SYSTEMS

JAN KAPLICKY Partner

Born Prague, Czechoslovakia   1937
College of Applied Arts and Architecture, Prague   1956–62
Private Practice   1962–8
Denys Lasdun & Partners   1969–71
Piano + Rogers   1971–3
Spencer & Webster   1973–4
Foster Associates   1977–83
Future Systems   1979–
Czech Chamber of Architects   1995–

AMANDA LEVETE Partner

Born Bridgend   1955
Architectural Association, London   1975–82
Alsop & Lyall   1980–1
YRM Architects   1982–4
Powis & Levete   1983–6
Richard Rogers Partnership   1984–9
Future Systems   1989–
Royal Institute of British Architects   1984–
ARB Board Member   1984–

DAVID MILLER Associate

Born Liverpool   1965
Leicester Polytechnic BA Hons Architecture   1983–6
Polytechnic of Central London Diploma in Architecture
1987–9
Foster Associates   1989–91
Calatrava Valls SA Paris   1992–5
Future Systems   1995

ANGUS POND Associate

Born London   1968
School of Architecture Portsmouth Polytechnic   1987–90
RMIT Melbourne Australia   1991
School of Architecture University of Portsmouth   1991–2
Nicholas Grimshaw & Partners   1990–3
Future Systems   1994

Dominic Harris   1976
Matthew Heywood   1970
Rachel Stevenson   1968

THANKS TO:

Peter Bell Brian Clarke Tony Danaher
Richard Davies Phillip Dodd Mark Emery
Marcus Field Paul Finch Norman Foster
Jonathan Glancey Jonathan Harper
Donna Harris Debra Hauer Tony Hunt
Adrian Joffe Michaela Kadnerova Rei
Kawakubo Jeremy King Bob Marshall
Andrews Gill Marshall Andrews Ann
Minogue Chris Newbold Jonathan
Newhouse Ronnie Newhouse Richard
Rogers Richard Schlagman Andy
Sedgwick Don Shuttleworth Mike Sindic
Jonathan Smales Wilf Stevenson
Maggie Toy Bill Tustin Matthew Wells
Henk Wiekens

2000

STRUCTURAL ENGINEERS

Anthony Hunt Associates
Dewhurst Macfarlane
Ove Arup & Partners
Techniker

ENVIRONMENTAL ENGINEERS

BDSP Partnership
Büro Happold
Ove Arup & Partners

QUANTITY SURVEYORS

Bucknall Austin
Davis Langdon & Everest
Hanscomb

COMPUTER IMAGES

Hayes Davidson

MODEL MAKERS

A Models
Arup Modelshop
Unit 22

PROJECT

191	**21st Century Gallery**	54–61
019	**45-Degree House**	34
017	**Archery Steps**	190
224	**The Ark**	26, 35, 110–17
01	**Attic Flat**	186
171	**Bibliothèque Nationale**	184, 193
135	**Blob**	181, 190
175	**Boatel**	36–7
254	**Bedford School**	160–1
186	**Caravan**	196
182	**Chiswick Park Entrance**	194
016	**Cockpit**	34
112	**Coexistence Tower**	181
256	**Comme des Garçons, New York**	
		26, 35, 162–5
257	**Comme des Garçons, Tokyo**	166–7
260	**Comme des Garçons, Paris**	168–9

02	**Concrete House**	186
246	**Construction Tower**	146–7
205	**Croydon Bridge**	68–9
219	**Docklands Bridge**	84–91
165	**Drop**	192
118	**DS Flat**	182, 189
232	**Electric Car**	130–1
10	**FD House and Studio**	187
249	**Flower Shop**	148–53
190	**Frankfurt Kindergarten**	196
196	**Furniture**	62–5
	Aluminium Table	64–5
	Anne's Cupboard	62
	Dinghy	63, 134
	Fauteuil	63
	Josef's Bed	62
	Wooden Table	64

PHOTOGRAPHERS

All photographs of Future Systems' Recent Projects 1990–2000 and models of Projects 1958–92 are by Richard Davies, with the exception of those listed below. Geoffrey Beeckman pp143, 144–5, 195, 205 John Clarke p4 Paul Harmer p132

INDEX

176	Green Bird	38–45
166	Green Building	192
240	Habitable Bridge	2–3, 138–41
242	Hallfield School	142–5
180	Hauer–King House	46–53
237	Hillgate Street	132–7
183	House at Berkhamsted	195
222	House in Wales	102–9, 179
178	Ivy Trolley	194
08	JD House and Garden	176, 186
216	Josef K House	74–7
113	Kew Gardens Centre Project	34
225	Linz Housing	118–9
221	Lord's Media Centre	16, 22, 92–101, 198
184	MOMI Tent	195
252	Mr B House	158–9
172	Museum of the Acropolis	184, 193

144	NASA Wardroom Table	191
124	Peanut	189
250	Prague Gardens	154–7
209	Prague Memorial	70–3
229	Project Zed, Berlin	126–9
226	Project Zed, London	120–3
228	Project Zed, Toulouse	124–5
139	Shelter	25, 185, 191
158	Spire	34
201	Stonehenge Visitors' Centre	197
203	Superbus	24, 66–7
218	Tate Gallery of Modern Art	82–3
192	Umweltschutzbehörde, Hamburg	197
133	'Way-In', Harrods	182, 190
005	Weekend Retreat for Miss B	190
217	Yokohama Port Terminal	78–81

Masayuki Hayashi   p167   Tony Hunt   p84   Hugh Hastings   pp164, 165
Nicolas Kane   p101   Ken Kirkwood   p188   Peter Mackinven   pp94, 98

future image

Josef Kaplicky 3 years